AN UNCOMMON BREWER

The Story of Whitbread

1742 ~ 1992

Stirring the coppers at the
Strangeways brewery in Manchester.

AN UNCOMMON BREWER

The Story of Whitbread

1742 ~ 1992

Berry Ritchie

JAMES
X
JAMES

DEDICATION

To all past, present and future members of the House of Whitbread in recognition of the debt that we owe to those who came before us and our responsibility to those who follow.

ACKNOWLEDGEMENTS

The author would like to record his thanks for their help to
Alex Bennett, Robin Farrington, Peter Jarvis, David Reed, Sir
Charles Tidbury, Colonel and Mrs Bill Whitbread, and Sam Whitbread.

Special mention is due to Nick Redman, Whitbread's archivist,
whose exemplary research laid the foundation for this book.

The Whitbread Archive, the largest organized collection of historic brewing
industry material in the country, is located at the Company's headquarters at
Chiswell Street, London.

First published in the UK in 1992 by
James & James (Publishers) Limited
75 Carleton Road, London N7 0ET

Copyright © 1992 Whitbread PLC

ISBN 0 907383 36 X

Editor Sydney Francis
Art director Ron Samuels
Text editor Conan Nicholas
Photographs of Whitbread pubs and breweries Alex Ramsay

Typeset by Bournetype Ltd, Bournemouth
Originated and printed in Great Britain by BAS Printers Limited, Over Wallop, Hampshire
Bound in Great Britain by Hunter & Foulis Ltd, Edinburgh

PICTURE ACKNOWLEDGEMENTS

Blackburn Library 115 *(bottom right)*; **Brewers' Hall** 94; **Bridgeman Art Library** 49 *(bottom)*, 56 *(top)*;
British Architectural Library/RIBA 60 *(bottom)*, 66 *(top)*, 73 *(bottom)*, 77 *(bottom, left and right)*, 102
(bottom), 118 *(bottom left and right)*; **British Museum** 17; **Courtauld Institute of Art** 24 *(bottom)*, 25, 36, 37
(top), 38 *(bottom)*, 54 *(bottom)*; **E T Archive** 71 *(top)*, 82; **Neil R. Gibbs, Spyglass Inn, Ventnor, Isle of
Wight** 68; **Guildhall Library** 26 *(bottom)*, 29 *(bottom)*; **Hulton Picture Company** 13 *(both)*, 16 *(top)*, 63 *(top)*;
Judges Postcards 89 *(bottom left)*; **Mary Evans** *half title*, 43 *(bottom)*; **Mansell Collection** 50 *(bottom)*, 51
(bottom), 66 *(bottom)*; **Peter Newark's Historical Pictures** 12, 48, 61 *(both)*, 70; **Alex Ramsay** *title page*, 6, 14,
15, 16 *(both)*, 17 *(both)*, 30 *(top left)*, 31, 33 *(bottom)*, 38 *(bottom)*, 45 *(both)*, 46, 52–3, 62 *(both)*, 75, 87, 88
(bottom), 98–9, 103 *(top left and bottom)*, 116 *(all)*, 120, 122 *(bottom)*, 124 *(both)*, 125, 126 *(all)*, 127 *(all)*, 129
(top), 130 *(top)*, 131 *(both)*, 134, 136 *(top right)*, 137 *(bottom)*, 141 *(bottom)*; **Ann Ronan Picture Library** 49
(top), 50 *(top)*, 54 *(top)*; **Searle Austin Associates** 141 *(top)*; **Mark Tillie** 38 *(top)*; **Uxbridge Arms,
London W8** 103 *(top right)*.

*All other pictures were photographed by Graham Tonks from the Whitbread Archive Collection and the premises
at Chiswell Street, or commissioned by Whitbread.*

CONTENTS

*The King Charles in Poole, Dorset, has
been a Whitbread pub for many years. Parts of
the building are over 550 years old and the pub
is the oldest in the town.*

FOREWORD

I am very proud of the fact that Whitbread is one of the few companies dating from the mid-eighteenth century not just to have survived, but to have become one of the top 100 companies in the United Kingdom while still maintaining a strong family involvement.

A number of common threads are woven through the story of the first 250 years of Whitbread.

The brewing industry seems to have been constantly in the political domain, with the anti-alcohol lobby's influence rising and falling. It is perhaps somewhat ironic that the first mention of a brewers' monopoly is as early as 1799.

From a business point of view, there seems never to have been a time when Whitbread did not have to manage its cash with extreme prudence. Generating enough money to fund its expansion plans emerges as a perennial challenge for the partners and directors, a difficulty perhaps eased by Whitbread's proximity, both physical and personal, to the City of London and its financial markets.

Another continuous theme running through the story is the conviction that social and commercial benefits go hand in hand. Whitbread has always believed that what is good for society as a whole is of benefit to the company. It is as true today as it was 250 years ago that our business can only thrive if the communities in which we trade are also flourishing.

But to me the most satisfying of these common threads is that of innovation. It is no exaggeration to claim that Whitbread has been innovating for two and a half centuries, from brewery design and the mass production of porter through the development of bottled beer in the 1860s to the introduction of lager, wine boxes and food retailing in modern times.

Whitbread is often seen as a traditional business. This does not mean we are an old-fashioned company. But there is a great deal to be said, I believe, for upholding traditional standards and values in the business world today. What will, I hope, keep Whitbread at the forefront of the British food and drink industry into the next century are our traditions of financial prudence, social responsibility and, above all, innovation.

Sam Whitbread

Electric transport was used extensively at
Chiswell Street from the 1920s to the 1940s. This
delivery was pictured leaving the North
Yard in 1921.

INTRODUCTION

In many ways, the story of Whitbread is a model of the British economy over the last 250 years.

Starting as a craft industry dependent on agriculture, Whitbread's methods were changed by the Industrial Revolution, changed again by Victorian scientific progress and have been transformed in the twentieth century by modern technology.

The evolution of Whitbread's business – the products it makes and the services it provides – has also faithfully reflected the avalanche of social change in the United Kingdom between 1742 and 1992.

Few companies have lasted for so long a period. Even fewer have emerged at the end among the leaders of their industry. If there is such an entity as a great British company, Whitbread is surely justified in laying claim to the title.

Why Whitbread should have survived and prospered is another question. Perhaps this, too, is because the character of the company has always mirrored national traits. Independent, insular, innovative, traditional, paternalistic, adventurous – all these adjectives apply to the history of Whitbread.

But on the other hand, perhaps they have nothing to do with it. Maybe the real secret of Whitbread's success is simply that it has always tried to brew good beer.

Berry Ritchie

This portrait of Samuel Whitbread I, painted by
Sir Joshua Reynolds in 1786–7, depicts the
great brewer in his middle sixties as a
determined, energetic personality, fully aware
of his status as a major landowner and
MP for Bedford Town, as well as a leading
figure in his industry.

CHAPTER ONE

FROM A VERY SMALL BEGINNING

1742–1758

Five years before his death, Samuel Whitbread wrote the first of a series of letters to his son about the family brewing business which he had founded in 1742.

'I will observe', he said in the course of the letter, 'that your father has raised it from a very small beginning and by great assiduity in a very long course of years and with the highest credit in every view by honest and fair dealings. And the beer universally approved and the quantity brewed annually great indeed.

'There never was the like before, nor probably ever will be again in the Brewing Trade.'

It was no more than the simple truth. At the age of 73 Samuel Whitbread was the greatest brewer in the United Kingdom, the sole owner of the largest and most famous brewery in perhaps the world, fabulously rich, and widely respected as much for his integrity as his achievements which were, as he was entitled to boast, entirely those of a self-made man.

Samuel Whitbread was born on 20 August 1720 in a comfortable family house called The Barns in Cardington, a village near Bedford, about 60 miles north of London. The family fortunes had survived the Civil War, when Whitbread's grandfather had fought for Oliver Cromwell, and as a second-generation Receiver-General for Taxes for the county of Bedfordshire his father Henry was comfortably off. Samuel was, however, the seventh of eight surviving children – five from a previous marriage. When his father died Samuel was only seven years old and his prospects were modest.

He was given two years' education by a clergyman in Northamptonshire and at 14 was sent to London, where he may have stayed with his step-brother Ive Whitbread, who had become a hardwareman in Cannon Street. Two years later the family paid John Wightman, Master of the

A pub in the eighteenth century depicted as a sociable and comfortable place, full of convivial gossip, warmth and wholesome beer.

Brewers' Company, to take him as an apprentice in his brewery in Clerkenwell, on the northern edge of the City.

The fee for the seven-year apprenticeship was £300. It was a substantial sum, comparable to the cost of sending someone through university today, which shows the value put on becoming a paid-up member of the Brewers' Company. Brewing had become a highly regarded profession by the 1730s, especially in London with its vast population of nearly three-quarters of a million to guarantee demand for what was a universal beverage. Almost everyone in the country drank beer and thought nothing of it. It was gin that was bad and those new-fangled drinks like tea and coffee.

John Wightman was one of London's Common Brewers, which meant he was a manufacturer who sold his beer wholesale to local public houses. By the time Samuel Whitbread started his apprenticeship, Common Brewers had a virtual monopoly of London's one and a half million barrel-a-year production, with the quantity home-brewed by publicans in their own cellars down to a tiny per cent. It was a trend that the Whitbread family was quite shrewd enough to see could only make brewing more profitable.

What the family most certainly did not realize, however, was that London beer production was on the verge of a revolution. Even John Wightman did not appreciate what was about to happen to his trade, although the seeds had been planted 14 years earlier.

Ralph Harwood, a partner in the Bell Brewhouse in Shoreditch, brewed his first batch of 'intire' or 'entire butt' beer in 1722. It was a strong, black beer whose first advantage seemed to be that it could be made from relatively cheap, coarse barley and robust, less-refined hops and was ideal for

London's soft water. Slightly scorched malt gave it a powerful, nourishing taste as well as its dark colouring. At first, however, its impurities made the beer cloudy and it appealed mainly to heavy manual workers such as food-market porters, who liked its body as much as the fact that it was cheap.

The real advantage of 'porter' took time to emerge. This was that it could be made in bulk, unlike lighter, clearer beers which deteriorated if matured in anything larger than a wooden cask. But for porter, the larger the container, the more complete the fermentation and the more 'entire' the utilization of the raw materials.

Harwood was not, apparently, very taken with the new beer, as he did not brew a great deal. Perhaps he was put off by the early problems of making porter less murky. At first the only answer was to mature it in casks for a few months. It was left to someone else to discover that a sprinkling of fishguts cleared the sediment. It also took time to learn that leaving porter to mature for a year or more improved it considerably. And even longer to appreciate that the greater the volume, the better and more economical the beer.

Harwood missed this point entirely. So did Wightman, along with most of the Brewers' Company. In fact, it wasn't until 1740, four years after Samuel Whitbread began his apprenticeship, that any brewer tried to take commercial advantage of porter's qualities by brewing it on a large scale.

There is no evidence that Samuel Whitbread was precociously perceptive, even though he took his apprenticeship seriously, unlike most of his contemporaries, which in itself is a guide to his character. London's

Taverns could also be haunts of vice, filled with dissolute gamblers and gin-drinkers.

Beer was transported in wooden casks by horse and dray, a method that limited distribution to local inns and taverns and put a natural economic boundary on how big most breweries could become.

apprentices were always notorious for their drinking and brawling, but in the first half of the eighteenth century they were especially dissolute and unbridled. An industrious one was rare enough to be the subject for a Hogarth sketch. Whitbread was admittedly lucky in having a master who did not treat him as cheap labour and his fees as cheap capital. Wightman obviously gave his apprentice a comprehensive insight into the mysteries of his trade. But Samuel was also clearly exceptionally self-disciplined.

Whitbread left Wightman's Gilport Street brewery seven months before the end of his apprenticeship. It was irregular but it did not debar him from becoming a freeman of the Brewers' Company in July 1743. By then he was in business on his own account and already no one doubted his abilities. Stocky, square-jawed and level-eyed, the young man from Bedford inspired confidence.

Samuel Whitbread went into partnership with Godfrey and Thomas Shewell on 11 December 1742. The value of the partnership was put at £14,116 and it comprised two small breweries; the larger, the Goat Brewhouse, on the corner of Old Street and Upper Whitecross Street, and the smaller on the other side of Old Street in Brick Lane, now renamed Central Street. The assets included 18 horses, 1,933 butts, 149 pipes, 293 punchions, 142 half-hogsheads, 200 kilderkins, 179 firkins and 5,036 feet of stillioning. Each brewery had a taphouse for retail sales and the firm also owned the leases of 14 local public houses. Loans to publicans, incidentally, totalling £9,405 at the date of purchase, made up an important part of the brewery's assets.

Whitbread's new partners were brothers whose father had been one of the previous owners of the Goat Brewhouse. They were, in effect, transferring their family business from one generation to the next. Neither, however, was a fully qualified brewer. Whereas Whitbread's election to the Brewers' Company was 'by service', Godfrey Shewell's membership, dating from the month before, was 'by purchase' and Thomas did not become a freeman until 1753. Whitbread, in other words, was being brought into the new partnership as the production expert – the term in current usage was managing partner.

Whitbread invested his patrimony of £2,000, raised another £600 by selling a small estate at Sodbury in Gloucestershire which he had inherited through his mother and borrowed the balance of his share of the cost of the partnership from family and friends in Bedfordshire to make a total investment at today's values of perhaps £250,000; a lot for a young man.

And then he went to work.

Hard work is one of the inevitable ingredients of any entrepreneurial success story. Quite what inspired such a devotion to his business in Samuel Whitbread is as hard to define as it is in any great businessman. His Puritan background had some influence. He was sincerely devout. His daughter Harriot described years later how her father never allowed 'the Sabbath to be broken into either in his counting-house, the yard, by travelling or dissipation'. And she also recorded that those who saw him with her and her brother Samuel II would have supposed he had nothing to do but attend to

The barn attached to Samuel Whitbread's birthplace at Cardington dates from about 1450. It has been restored by Whitbread and converted into a function room for the Barns Hotel.

them. But she added that those who knew him in his brewhouse yard or counting-house only thought he had his trade as his first and last object. 'When the rest of the world were asleep, he entered on the worldly business of the day.'

For the new managing partner of the Goat Brewhouse, the day was all too short. For a start Whitbread was his own chief brewer.

Making beer was still a 'mystery', with its quality depending on the empirical skills of individual brewers. Although the search for scientific methods of making beer had begun, no one, not even the members of the Brewers' Company, understood the chemical principles. Master brewing was much more like cordon bleu cooking, requiring a combination of flair and care. In the early part of his trade, Harriet wrote, 'he sat up four nights a week by his brewhouse copper, refreshing himself by washing plentifully with cold water and, when the state of the boiling permitted his quitting, retired for two hours to his closet reading the Scriptures and devotional exercise.'

Samuel Whitbread was born at The Barns in Cardington, near Bedford, the second of three children from his father's second marriage, to Elizabeth Winch. This comfortable family home was sold to Trinity College in the 1890s, but was bought back by Whitbread in 1988. It is now a hotel.

Brewing in the sixteenth century, showing processes that have remained unchanged over 400 years. When Samuel Whitbread was learning the brewing trade, it was still using similar labour-intensive methods. Today, the industry is technologically more sophisticated, but the principles remain the same. (From a woodcut by J. Ammon.)

But actually brewing beer was only a small part of the business. To begin with the raw materials had to be acquired. Whitbread was hiring his own maltings at Hitchin as early as 1748, but in the early years he bought most of his malt from a maltster called Charles Brown. He bought hops through a Southwark factor in the same way. One of the advantages of merchants was the use of their warehouses, but in any case production of malt and hops was traditionally separate from brewing. One good reason was that crops could vary wildly from year to year – which meant so did prices. Samuel Whitbread paid £4,200 for hops in the year to the end of September 1747, only £1,600 the following year, £5,440 the year after that and down again to £2,970 in 1749/50. With the sale price of beer effectively fixed, the brewery's margins were very vulnerable to these variations in the price of supplies and Samuel had to be constantly alert to market changes.

He was also responsible for another marketing aspect of the brewery, the sale of spent grains and surplus yeast. Most of London's bread was made with brewer's yeast; so was much of the gin distilled in the capital. And almost all the capital's cows and pigs, kept in dark, noisome pounds, were fed on brewer's grains – there is nothing new about factory farming.

Less entrepreneurial but equally demanding was the day-to-day business of the brewery, such as barrel manufacture and maintenance, and the distribution of the beer to its customers. Horses were a major expense for a brewery. Whitbread's annual bills to smiths, farriers, wheelwrights and collarmakers in 1748/9 were £200 with as much again for hay, straw, oats, beans and bran. The drayhorses themselves cost about £16 each and had a working life of up to 15 years. The poor mill horses were seldom worth more than £5.

This engraving from the Universal Magazine of 1748/9 shows contemporary brewing in detail. **A** *is the big copper heated by the furnace,* **C**. **D** *is described as a mash-vat or tub and* **E** *is the mashing oar. Below this,* **F** *is a receiver or under-vat and, at the top,* **B** *is a 'rudder, lead or pump' to pump up the wort out of the receiver into the copper to boil. On the floor,* **G** *shows two ladles, one with a long and one with a short handle.* **H** *marks the coolers and* **I** *is a pump at the back of the copper that fills it with cold water. The water from* **I** *is also used to wash the casks,* **K**, *as well as the working tubs, tuns and barrels.*

Coopering in the eighteenth century. The art of coopering continued at Whitbread until wooden barrels were replaced by metal ones in the 1960s.

And then there was the whole question of customer relations. Although the Goat Brewhouse owned the leases of 14 pubs, the business was not based on them – but admittedly they had been acquired to maintain beer sales. All the pubs were held on intermediary leases, with the receipts of £377 a year barely matching the annual rents to the head leaseholders of £375. After paying for repairs and maintenance, Whitbread and his partners were losing money. They only took over the leases reluctantly, when the tenants got into financial difficulties or wanted to leave. In 1750, for example, they paid the retiring tenant of the Sun in Temple Court, William Joslyn, a premium of £28 for his lease, plus another £12 for his furniture. In his place they installed their own tenant, Paul Cockton, at a yearly rent of £26, which was £4 more than the cost of the head lease. The margin was too small to make economic sense, but the choice was to allow the pub to fall into the hands of a competing brewer. The seeds of the 'tied-house' system were already planted.

None of the brewers regarded owning pubs as anything but a necessary evil. The profits came from beer sales, of which by far the larger proportion was to free houses.

In the first year under Whitbread's management, total production was 18,000 barrels, a not unimpressive total for the time, with the Goat Brewhouse making porter and 'small beer', and the Brick Lane brewhouse

WHITBREAD PUBS TODAY
The George Inn at Southwark, on the south bank of the River Thames in London, was rebuilt in its present form after a fire in 1676, but there has been an inn on the site since 1542. An important coaching-inn on the main road over London Bridge, it was similar to many supplied by Samuel Whitbread and his partners when they began brewing porter in 1742. The George, the only galleried inn left in London, has been a Whitbread pub since 1962.

pale and amber beers. And within five years the firm had run out of space for horses and drays and was hiring cellars in 54 different places to store maturing output.

This alone is evidence that Whitbread had 'discovered' porter. He was not the first. In 1748 Sir William Calvert brewed 55,700 barrels of what was still called strong beer and his brother John was not far behind with 53,600 barrels. Benjamin Truman was third with 39,400 barrels and between them the first twelve breweries in London produced 383,000 barrels out of a total of 915,000 barrels. Already the economies of scale implicit in porter production were making themselves apparent.

But no one saw the potential more clearly than Whitbread. We must, he told his partners, expand. Godfrey Shewell demurred, pulled out his capital and joined another brewer. Undeterred, Samuel and Thomas borrowed more money and bought the derelict King's Head Brewhouse and a row of adjoining tenements along the south side of Chiswell Street, not far from Old Street. By 1750 they had demolished the whole site and built a new brewery specifically designed for the mass production of porter.

By the end of his life, Samuel Whitbread's Chiswell Street Brewery was one of the wonders of London, a staggering production and distribution complex filled with the very latest steam-powered technology, visited by royalty and famous throughout the land. But this was after more than 40 years' expansion and development. In 1750 the new brewery was no more than a state-of-the-art version of other 'Great Common Brewhouses' built in the previous ten years to produce porter. However, by previous standards, this still made the new Chiswell Street brewery a large industrial development.

Size was quite literally the important difference. The technique for making beer remained essentially the same as it had been for centuries. What had changed was the scale – both in the volume of materials and the plant itself. As the *London Brewer* explained in 1742, the year that Samuel Whitbread set up in business, 'in erecting a large work of this kind, everything is to be considered that can save the labour of the people involved, for as everything is done in quantities, the difficulty of removing the ingredients from place to place would be very great, but for the help of such early care'.

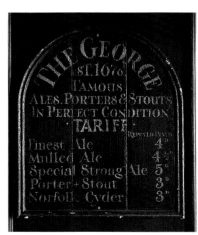

The Porter Tun-Room at Chiswell Street, completed in 1784, was originally built as a storehouse. This drawing shows casks in the vaults that were later converted into cisterns.

Hogarth's Gin Lane cartoon of 1751 is a cruel depiction of the evils of gin-drinking, a habit that was widespread among England's working classes during the first half of the eighteenth century.

Ideally, this meant what by Georgian standards was a high-rise building. The top floor of the new Chiswell Street brewery was a large, airy space slatted against sunlight and containing the coppers in which the malted barley was boiled. The coppers were placed in pairs, so that one stoker could fuel two at a time from a single coal store and, in this 'great' new brewhouse, they were at least 11 feet above ground level. Once they had done their work, the 'wort' they had created was run off through a false bottom which trapped the used hops into shallow cooling-pans or 'squares', and then down again into the 'great working tuns' to ferment with the aid of yeast. Finally, the new beer was run off into storage casks to mature in underground vats. All it took was horse-driven treadmills to grind the malt and pump water from the brewery's own well to the top of the new brewery, and gravity provided the rest of the energy needed.

Technologically, Chiswell Street was no different from the Goat Brewhouse. Economically, however, Samuel Whitbread and Thomas Shewell had moved into another league entirely.

One of the aspects of the new brewery which did mark it out was the high quality of its construction. This alone was evidence that the partners were taking a long-term view of their business, although it might just have reflected the fact that they owned the freehold. Most buildings in London at the time were incredibly shoddy. 'Falling houses thunder on your head', Samuel Johnson wrote in 1738. A major reason was poor land titles, as well as badly made bricks. Whitbread, however, had an instinctive commitment to quality as well as quantity.

The dynamism of London may also have convinced him that its population was growing, but if so it was a subjective impression. Although there was a constant flow of immigrants from the country, the total population of the metropolis in 1750 at 676,000 was no more than it had been 50 years earlier. If anything, the number of people living in London in the previous 30 years had fallen, due to an extraordinarily high death rate and low birth rate. The reason was gin.

England was in the grip of an orgy of spirit drinking between 1720 and 1750. A representation to the House of Commons in 1751 on the effects of cheap gin estimated that they included the deaths each year in London alone of more than 9,000 children under five. 'Other trivial reasons (like poor diet and sanitation) for this great mortality may possibly require some abatement, but the real grand destroyer is materially evident.'

It certainly was. The cause had been official encouragement for distilling, a new trade in England in the late seventeenth century, because it gave farmers a market for cereals and was supposed to help the balance of trade. It certainly helped some of England's biggest landowners become inordinately rich. Distillers and retailers of spirits were almost entirely untaxed and uncontrolled.

By the time Samuel arrived in London, the effects of unlimited gin sales had become so appalling that action was about to be taken. However, the 1736 Gin Act, which tried to tax the retail trade out of business, turned out to be unenforceable and was repealed seven years later. When Whitbread

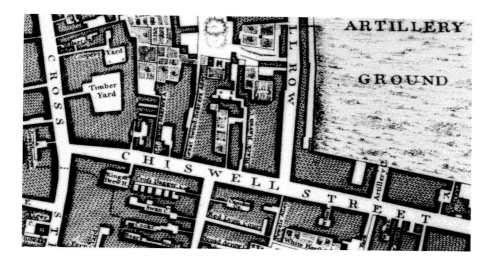

John Rocque's map of London, published in 1746, shows the King's Head brewhouse in Chiswell Street. Bought by Samuel Whitbread in 1748, the brewhouse was pulled down to make room for the new brewery, which eventually became the largest in the country.

and Shewell moved to Chiswell Street, the gin trade was once again out of control.

But people had had enough. Protests, including Hogarth's scathing Gin Lane cartoons and Henry Fielding's *Reasons for the late Increase of Robbers*, brought acts of parliament in 1751, which stopped distillers selling retail or to unlicensed publicans, and in 1753, which gave magistrates more control and introduced annual licences. Between them, these new laws cut gin consumption by three-quarters.

The brewers benefited twice over. The 'universal approval' of beer as a healthy, wholesome drink suitable for all the family was reinforced and the population began to increase in leaps and bounds. Every good businessman deserves some luck. Whitbread's was timing. He couldn't have chosen a more perfect moment at which to open a brand-new brewery dedicated to the mass production of beer.

Luck did not come into his decision to make porter, however. That was a combination of technical and commercial intelligence. In 1750 porter had become the staple drink in the metropolis. It was retailing everywhere in London at 3d. per quart pot, a third cheaper than most other beers and the same price it had been for nearly 30 years. There was no question of brands and brewery prices were as fixed as the retail price at 23s. per barrel, leaving the publicans who bought it a 13s. a barrel profit margin. With demand assured, all Whitbread and Shewell had to guarantee was consistent quality and supply.

The only unfixed element in the business sum was the cost of production. It was here that economies of scale came into their own. As the two partners were discovering, the more porter they brewed at Chiswell Street, the more completely the mash absorbed the raw materials and the less malt and hops were needed for the same strength of beer. It gave them the marvellous ability to compete on price or on strength. It was an advantage Sam Whitbread exploited to the full. Within eight years production at Chiswell Street was nearly 65,000 barrels and Whitbread & Shewell had overtaken the Calvert brothers and Ben Truman to become the largest firm of porter brewers in London.

Beer Street, also drawn by Hogarth in 1751, is much kinder than Gin Lane. Beer, which almost everyone in the country drank, was regarded as a safe, healthy and nutritious beverage.

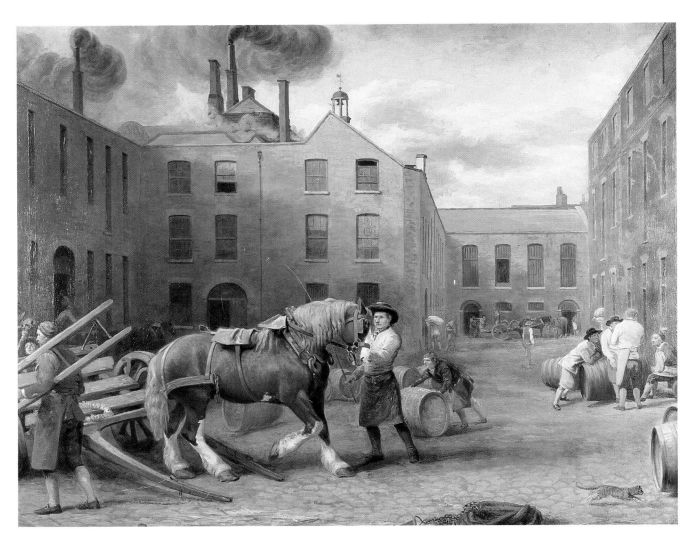

*The South Yard at Chiswell Street, painted by
George Garrard in 1792. On the left is the
Great Storehouse (later the Porter Tun-Room)
and next to that the brewery.*

CHAPTER TWO

NEVER THE LIKE BEFORE

1758–1796

Samuel Whitbread and Thomas Shewell were delighted with their achievement in becoming London's largest brewers. It made 1758 an historic year which they undoubtedly toasted in their own beer.

Surprisingly, their rapid rise up the production league table appears to have been unopposed. Sir William Calvert, for example, was brewing no more than he had ten years previously and John Calvert had raised his output by a mere 8,000 barrels. Even Truman had only managed to increase production by 16,000 barrels a year.

There were two reasons. One was flat demand. Sales of beer in London hardly changed in the decade, although 1758 did see an upturn after five successive falls. The other, which may have reflected the former or been the reason for it, was the failure of other brewers to increase their own capacity. Eight years on, Chiswell Street was still the largest brewery in the metropolis, which was either a tribute to the scale on which it had been planned or a comment on the attitude of Whitbread's competitors to investing in new plant and equipment.

It would be wrong to blame them for caution. Half a century of static prices and sales volume was hardly the basis for a business philosophy based on the assumption of future growth.

Even Whitbread and Shewell levelled off in the next few years. Output in 1760 was down to 63,400 barrels and two years later it fell again to 55,000 barrels.

By then it was just Samuel Whitbread. Thomas Shewell had decided to retire at the end of the previous financial year and his partner had arranged to buy him out for £30,000, payable in instalments between 1765 and 1770. The price was a handsome measure of how far the partnership had come in its 19 years.

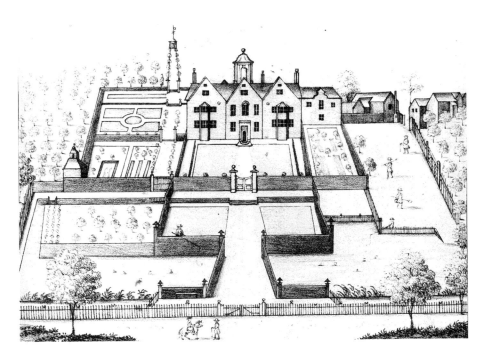

An engraving of Bedwell Park from Chauncey's History of Hertfordshire (1700). The house and park were bought by Samuel Whitbread in 1765.

Joseph Delafield was 38 when this portrait was painted by George Romney in 1787. Delafield joined the brewery in 1764.

As well as buying out his old partner, Whitbread had also felt confident enough to borrow £4,450, 'as I could not spare it to be taken out of Trade', to pay for a small estate at Cardington. 'I bought at Cardington', he wrote in his property book, 'because it was the place of my birth and inheritance of my father, and as it has pleased God to bless me with great abundance . . . I have all along in life thought it my duty to show some token of gratitude to almighty God, who maketh poor and rich, in the place where I was born by improving the parish where our family lived 150 years.'

Over the next 27 years Whitbread spent £60,000 on building up a landed estate at Cardington, although he confessed just before his death that he valued it at only £50,000 as he considered that he had spent £10,000 in superfluities. 'And I had a pleasure in so doing.'

He also bought Ion House at nearby Shidlington 'because it was in the parish where the Whitbreads had lived before they moved to Cardington in 1639'. It was equally, of course, an investment. As he became progressively richer, Whitbread's property holdings became steadily larger until at the end of his life his various estates covered 12,000 acres, including his own home of Bedwell Park in Hertfordshire, bought in 1765 for £8,000, and Southill in Bedfordshire, which he purchased shortly before his death as a country seat for his son. By the time he had finished, Samuel Whitbread's estates were worth in the region of £400,000, equal to perhaps £8 million at today's values. And all, as he stressed to his son, bought out of the profits of the brewery. 'The fortune that you will enjoy was not obtained by avaricious savings, for I have spent plentifully and enlarged my expenses as my fortune increased, nor on a sudden by the Stocks, nor Contracts, nor Speculations, nor Legacys. But in this one regular branch of Trade only.'

Again, it was nothing but the truth. At the mature age of 38, Samuel had married Harriot Hayton and the same year their daughter, named after her mother, was born. It was this event which inspired his interest in building up a family estate. But it was still the brewery which absorbed most of Whitbread's energies.

For most of the next ten years, he worked as hard as ever. It was this period that his daughter remembered, when the family was living in the dwelling-house attached to the brewery, rebuilt in 1756 for £1,000, perhaps in anticipation of his marriage. This only lasted for six years. In 1764 his first wife died after bearing him a son. Five years later Whitbread married again, this time to Lady Mary Cornwallis, sister of the general whom history remembers for surrendering to the American rebels at Yorktown in 1781. Sadly this marriage, too, ended in her death in childbirth a year later, leaving Samuel with another daughter.

By then he was 50, old enough to want to take life easily and wealthy enough to do so in style. Instead, his interest in his business renewed itself.

Samuel Whitbread's marriage to Lady Mary, daughter of Earl Cornwallis, can only be described as a turning point in his life. It is incontrovertible evidence that he was a 'made man'. In the 21 years since its purchase, the Chiswell Street brewery had made him rich. The 1760s had been particularly rewarding, with profits averaging £18,000 a year on production which had gradually risen to 90,000 barrels in 1769.

By then he had honed the brewery into an efficient operation which could run itself, enabling him to adopt a lifestyle suitable to the husband of an earl's daughter, split between a town house in Portman Square, his country seat at Bedwell Park and visits to fashionable spas like Bath. Among his business talents, Samuel Whitbread possessed perhaps the most valuable of all, that of being able to get the best out of his employees. It was something he was very proud of. 'I have also had in conducting this business', he wrote to his son in 1791, 'the best set of Clerks and that have lived the longest with one Master, as is not to be met with anywhere else. I have kept a list of them which I desire you to commit to your posterity.'

The list contained 12 names. All but one had begun to work for him before 1769. The earliest were William Slater, who had started work for Whitbread in 1743, and Broughton Maysey, who had joined the firm in 1747. Maysey was the closest. 'He represented me when absent upon all occasions and for many years drew himself upon the Bank for all my Cash. I trusted him until he chose to resign it.' Latterly, his role had been filled by Jacob Yallowley, who had started work in 1760, and Robert Sangster, who had become an employee in 1764, along with Joseph Delafield.

Maysey also took over responsibility for buying malt and hops in the 1770s, helped by Sangster. Samuel Green, who began work in 1752, was in charge of brewing, 'as he has done for years and most thoroughly understands it in all respects', assisted by David Jennings, who had joined seven months later and was also a 'perfect master of it'.

The last name on the list, a latecomer in 1772, was Elijah Pryce, of whom Whitbread wrote 'he is the first collecting clerk and a very faithful intelligent man, very proper for his situation and filled it now for twenty years'. Collecting debts was, then as always, a business essential.

Samuel Green, the head brewer, joined Whitbread in 1752, two years after the move to Chiswell Street. Here he is aged 55, painted by Thomas Gainsborough in 1781.

Fires were a continual hazard during the brewery's early years, sometimes put out with the liquid to hand – porter.

Between them, this team of clerks, who today would be called managers or even executives, freed Samuel to take a more strategic role. There was scope for it. The fact was that the original development of the Chiswell Street site had remained virtually unchanged for 20 years, although a cooperage with a house for the head cooper, some stables and a retail beershop had been built in 1758, and a new storehouse and an extension to the tun-room had been added in 1760. The time had come for expansion.

The first burst of redevelopment was inspired by a fire in 1773 which, although it was put out by £500 worth of beer which burst out of one of the vats, destroyed the old porter tun-room.

Whitbread built a new storehouse with enlarged vaults underneath – the first stone, he noted proudly, was laid by ten-year-old Samuel junior. This was followed by improvements to the taphouse and a rebuild for the counting-house which incorporated a new gateway, plus a large connection to the City's new sewer along Chiswell Street. And in 1776 there was a whole rash of improvements: an addition to the Long Stable, accompanied by underpinning and the deepening of the vaults below by seven feet; a building across the east end of the Great Yard; two vaults under the yard; and more building at the end of the Great Storehouse. All this was followed in 1777 by yet more stabling and, the finishing touch, paving for the Great Yard.

The enlarged vaults released a hitherto dormant interest in new technology. Gazing at their freshly cut stone walls, Whitbread wondered how to make best use of them.

> My first thought was upon Vats, but at length a very singular idea occurred to my mind and that was to fill a part of the Vaults themselves with Beer . . . which I apprehended would certainly be making the most of the room and from their situation in the earth be beneficial beyond any Cask whatever to the quality of the Beer, and attended with less Fermentation than Casks which are more exposed to the Air and on the whole admit of a longer length in the Beer brewed from an equal quantity of Malt and Hops when kept in Casks. Which have all turned out as first conjectured.

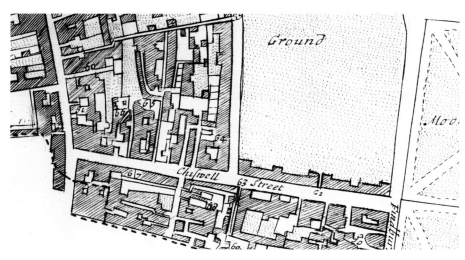

Strype's map of the area around Chiswell Street in 1755.

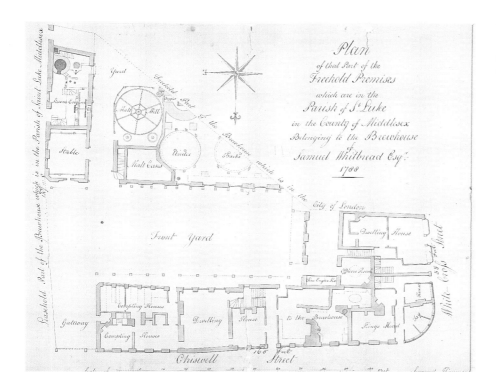

The earliest plan of the brewery, drawn in 1788, shows part of the premises on the south side at Chiswell Street (north is at the bottom of the map).

But not without trials and tribulations. Whitbread first hired Robert Mylne, the architect of the new Blackfriars Bridge. Mylne was confident that plaster made with Dutch trass would be an adequate waterproofing – so confident that he promised to stand under the vault when it was full. 'But when filled only with water the force was so great that it ran through all the walls as though through a sieve. I paid off Mr Mylne with a Bank Note for £20 in a letter and took it in hand ourselves,' Samuel noted dismissively.

John Smeaton, the engineer who designed the third Eddystone lighthouse and was responsible for improving navigation on the River Lea and, more intimately, for building Samuel a bridge over a stream on his Cardington land, tried next. He proposed York stone of the kind used for London's footpaths, bonded with a cement of rosin, beeswax and sand. The corrosive powers of beer proved more than a match for this solution.

Whitbread then wrote to Josiah Wedgwood to ask if he thought special glazed tiles would work and to Matthew Boulton of the construction engineers Boulton & Watt for suggestions about acid-proof cement. Ship's caulkers were hired to fill the joints between the stones with white lead, linseed and sand. Tinned copper plates were put over all the angles. Iron ties and buttresses combated the pressure on the walls. Still the stone cisterns leaked.

Stubbornly, Whitbread persisted, building a second and a third giant cistern. Each one leaked. Gradually the problems were overcome, although it took nearly ten years before the vaults were entirely water-, or rather beer-tight, by which time they had cost over £7,000. But between them they could hold 12,000 barrels and they did, Whitbread was delighted to discover, have all the economic advantages that he had hoped.

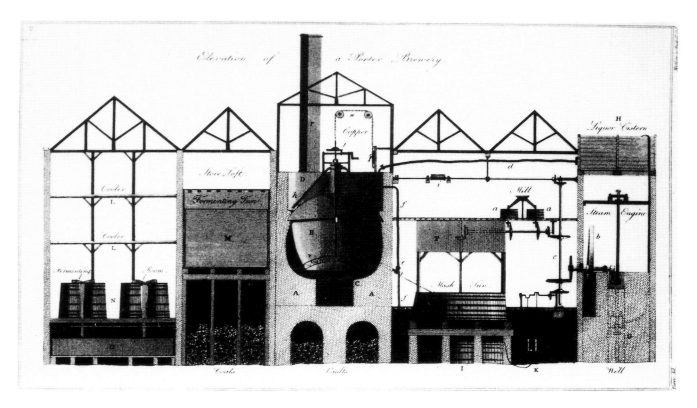

This illustration of the vessels and the elevation of the porter brewery is taken from drawings made by J. Farey in Chiswell Street, and published in Pantalogia – A New Encyclopedia, 1813. The brewing techniques are the same as shown on page 16. The Boulton & Watt steam engine is on the right of the drawing.

It was an experience that might have blunted his enthusiasm for new ideas, especially as he was naturally a traditionalist. He never, for example, showed much interest in scientific aids to assessing the strength of beer which were beginning to appear, such as thermometers and hydrometers. But maybe that was because he preferred to keep beer-making a mystery; after all, he had a good brewer and there was no percentage in simplifying the process so that everyone could do it.

He was quick enough to seize on new inventions when the economic advantages of using them were stronger. Such as steam power, which Whitbread only narrowly failed to be the first brewer to order. (He was beaten by one month by Henry Goodwyn, whose order was dated May 1784. The next, from Felix Calvert, was 16 months later.)

The arrival of a Boulton & Watt steam engine to grind malt and pump water up to the boilers at Chiswell Street was chronicled by Joseph Delafield in a letter to his brother dated 1 March 1786. 'It is built in the place where the mill horses used to stand,' he wrote. 'You may remember our wheel required six horses but we ordered our engine with the power of ten and the work it does we think equal to fourteen horses, for we grind with all our four mills about 40 quarters an hour beside raising the liquor. We began this season's work with it and have now ground about 28,000 quarters with it without accident or interruption.' The engine, Delafield added, had enabled the brewery to dispense with 24 horses which had each been costing at least £40 per annum, almost equal to the £1,000 the engine had cost to install. 'It consumes only a bushel of coals an hour, and we pay an annual gratuity to Bolton (*sic*) and Watt during their patent of £60.'

Delafield told his brother that to give a particular description of the engine would reach rather beyond the limits of a letter, but such was his enthusiasm that he tried anyway.

Know that from a close Boiler of Water the Steam passes thro' a Neck from the top of it, to the top of a perpendicular Cylinder in which works a Piston, which Piston (an air pump previously making a stroke and obtaining a Vacuum in the Cylinder) is forced to the bottom (6 feet) by the Steam – more steam is then introduced under the Piston which then forces it up again, which Steam then passes down a pipe standing in a Cistern of cold water, is met by a small portion of it admitted thro' a Valve fixed on the side of the pipe, which condensing the steam is pump'd away in warm Water the Piston being fasten'd to a Beam working on its centre of course moves t'other end up and down and turns the Mills.

He had already told his brother about other 'mighty works' at the brewery, including new tuns and coppers, which had raised production the previous year to 143,000 barrels. He went on to describe the plans for the coming summer, which involved pulling down three recently bought houses on White Cross Street, a road off Chiswell Street, and building a new tun-room in their place. 'The Brewhouse, as the possession of an individual is and will be when it is finished still more so, the wonder of everybody – by which means our pride is become very troublesome, being almost daily resorted to by Visitors, either Friends or Strangers.'

Whitbread's Chiswell Street brewery was, in truth, becoming a marvel of its time. The ultimate accolade came the following year with a royal visit. 'The facts are these', Delafield wrote to his brother on 2 June 1787:

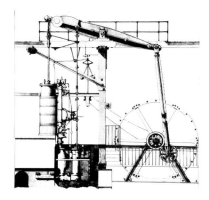

The Boulton & Watt steam engine was installed in the brewery in 1785. It was used by Whitbread for over a hundred years, being replaced in 1887. The machine was not destroyed, however, but exported to Australia. Now it is in Sydney, in the Power House Museum of Applied Arts and Sciences.

Another view of the South Yard by George Garrard, this time in 1783, looking eastwards and showing the Great Storehouse on the right.

WHITBREAD PUBS TODAY
In this late nineteenth-century photograph (*right*) of the King's Head tap-house in Chiswell Street, the building has not changed much from when it was rebuilt by Whitbread in 1750. Early this century, the façade was altered to look very much as it does today (*far right*).

The visit of King George III and the royal family to Mr Whitbread's brewery in Chiswell Street in 1787 was an important event. This stone tablet, built into the wall on the south side of Chiswell Street, commemorates the visit.

THEIR MAJESTIES
KING GEORGE III & QUEEN CHARLOTTE
WERE RECEIVED IN THIS BREWERY
BY
SAMUEL WHITBREAD
24ᵗʰ MAY 1787

About ten days ago we had information that they would come last Saturday (26 May) & the preparations and Honors of the day were committed by the Father entirely to Miss Whitbread both in the Brewhouse and Dwelling where she conducted with great Spirit and management. On the Brewho' we ceased work and began cleaning on Friday morning & spread matting all thro' the House where they were to walk – the Walls adjoining being lined with [here the letter is torn] . . . Horses all in the Stables and Men in the Yard – the Engine (the best piece of mechanism I thought I ever saw) and House made clean and handsome – the Great Vaults being shut from daylight were lighted with rows of Patent Lamps. . . . One of the Great Cisterns that holds near 4,000 barrels being empty was also lighted by a number of small lamps along the springing and round the circle of the arch, and exhibited a very extraordinary and pleasing effect. Thus prepared in the Brewhouse and in the Dwellinghouse, Miss Whitbread having set out a very elegant Breakfast Table with Fruits, Wines etc before ten o'clock on Saturday morning, came the King, Queen, Princess Royal, Princesses Augusta and Elizabeth with the Duchess of Ancaster and Lady Harcourt, the Duke of Montague and Lord Aylesbury. They were received by Mr and Miss Whitbread at the Brewhouse door next the Dwelling and immediately after myself and Mr Yallowley joined and waited on them through the whole Premises, in which they staid (*sic*) until half past Twelve – highly entertained and pleased with the magnitude and order of the place of

which they had not any conception – and wonderfully pleased was the King with the Engine. They staid an hour afterwards in the Dwelling and upon the whole by their agreeable and easy manners and conduct shew'd themselves to be highly entertained and afforded high honor and pleasure to all who attended them.

The visit was one of the high points of Samuel Whitbread's career, a formal recognition that he was the country's leading brewer. It was a status already accorded him by his competitors, of whom the closest were still the Calverts and Truman, plus the merged firm of Henry Thrale and Barclay Perkins. Under the impetus of the continuing improvements at Chiswell Street, the Whitbread brewery gradually stretched its lead over its rivals until 1796, when it became the first to produce over 200,000 barrels in a single year, a third more than its nearest competitor.

In spite of his pre-eminence, Samuel Whitbread's final years were clouded with one regret. His son, he knew, was not the man to succeed him.

The knowledge that Samuel junior was not interested in following in his father's footsteps had been in the back of Whitbread's mind for years, but he finally came to terms with it. 'I have long since intended to have known your mind upon this subject of trade if I could possibly have obtain'd it of you, viz. if you had any idea of carrying it on,' he wrote to his son, adding sadly, I now waive it. . . . So very clear I am that you should not have any thought of continuing the trade, I intend to dispose of it myself and save you that trouble. This is my intention if it please God I live.' The letter was dated 9 November 1791. The following April he thought he had found a buyer. 'I am now preparing myself to dispose of it at Michaelmas next, before the next Brewing Season, and shall apply to Mr Harvey of Norwich, who wrote me a letter Jany. 24. 1789.'

The news that the great Chiswell Street brewery was on the market spread and in July 1792 Samuel Whitbread received another approach, this time from an acquaintance called Smith, backed by two other businessmen, Sumner and Leicester. 'I have tho't much on it since & conclude it is not unlikely,' Whitbread confided. 'Sumner's eldest son is a man of business, Leicester is a very honest proper man and has sons and Smith a son. They have wealth and good characters and I shall talk seriously to them soon. Sumner, Smith & Leicester and have Yallowley, Green Sangster added to them would do the business and be an extraordinary good firm or partnership.'

The stumbling-block was the value Whitbread put on his brewery and porter business of £300,000. Smith and his friends could not raise the capital. Nor could the Harveys – or at least, Harvey senior, a retired banker, could not bring himself to commit his capital, much as his three sons begged him to. The eldest, Robert, was particularly keen, as his letters to Whitbread revealed. But although the correspondence dragged on until April 1795, in the end the deal came to nothing.

In the final analysis, Samuel Whitbread was to blame for the failure. There was no shortage of people willing to pay handsomely for a partnership

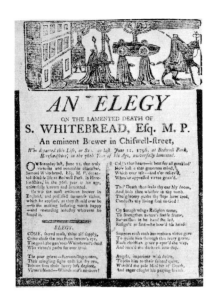

An elegy on the death of Samuel Whitbread, printed during the week following his demise on Saturday, 11 June 1796.

in the brewery. For Whitbread, though, it was all or nothing. Quite simply, he could not bring himself to share his life's work with anyone else.

He did not live to see its crowning as the first to brew 200,000 barrels. He died on 11 June 1796 at Bedwell Park worth 'a million at least' according to the *Gentleman's Magazine*, which remembered him as a man 'whose abilities, integrity, benevolence and public spirit will transmit his character with respect to the latest posterity'.

It was a justified obituary. Samuel Whitbread was a model capitalist, a prototype for those whom the Industrial Revolution was beginning to create, incorporating all the best virtues of the class.

In his later years Whitbread had become a public figure. He had been elected an MP for Bedford town in 1768 and sat in the House of Commons with one short break until his death. His political ambitions were modest. A natural Tory, he discharged his parliamentary duties in much the same spirit that he sat on the local Bench, as an accepted responsibility for a wealthy man, and he was in no sense a radical. But he made a name for himself as a supporter of prison reform, advocated by his childhood friend John Howard, and of the abolition of slavery. He was, wrote his daughter, really the first man to mention the slave trade in the House of Commons.

He also gave generously to John Howard's prison reform campaign and towards the founding of hospitals and charity schools. He was especially shocked to learn that London hospitals discharged incurable cancer patients and funded a ward in the Middlesex Hospital for their care which survives to this day.

His fame, however, rested on his achievement in becoming the greatest brewer in the land, and his most lasting monument was the 'mighty works' he had wrought at Chiswell Street.

The brewery's logo of a hind's head was taken from Samuel Whitbread's coat of arms.

This monument to Samuel Whitbread was commissioned by his son for St Mary's Church, Cardington, Bedfordshire, shortly after the father's death. John Bacon, the sculptor, tried to increase by 200 guineas the 'utmost limit' of 1,300 guineas on the cost of the monument, but finally agreed to the original figure. The inscription was written by Samuel Whitbread II.

*James Northcote's posthumous (1816) portrait
of Samuel Whitbread II incorporating Garrard's
1792 view of the South Yard at Chiswell Street.*

CHAPTER THREE

A VERY LARGE FORTUNE

1796–1815

The relationship between Whitbread and his son was complex and contradictory. In their different ways they loved each other, but they were never comfortable. To the young Samuel, his father was reactionary, puritanical and dictatorial. To the father, his only male offspring seemed naïve and awkward.

In fact, the young Whitbread possessed a strong character and considerable intellect, as his parliamentary career was to reveal. What he had not inherited was his father's flair for business. Not that he ever had the chance to develop one. Sam I made the classic mistake of giving his son the education that he had lacked himself.

In Sam II's case, this meant Eton and Cambridge (and, apparently, Oxford as well, although only briefly). Whitbread junior proved to be an able scholar. He also made aristocratic and, as his father perceived them, dangerously liberal friends, such as Charles Grey, the future Whig prime minister.

After college, young Sam was sent on the Grand Tour of Europe, as mandatory for well-off young men at the end of the eighteenth century as round-the-world backpacking has become for middle-class youth of today. Unlike his contemporaries, however, Whitbread junior's itinerary, drawn up by his father, included the cold, character-building countries of Denmark, Sweden, Russia, Poland and Prussia, as well as France and Italy. If Samuel I had hoped that the experience would predispose his son to work in the brewery, he was disappointed. When Sam II returned to England in 1787, it was already obvious that he was not going to follow in his father's footsteps.

To Whitbread's credit, he accepted it. 'My Dear Son,' he wrote, 'You will have a very large fortune and not be in want of any improvement of it. Any concern of Trade would be a burthen to you. Therefore I beseech again don't think of continuing it. But sell it.'

Jacob Yallowley, aged 57, painted by George Romney in 1787. Yallowley was one of the 'loyal clerks', having been with Whitbread since 1760.

Easier said than done, as the founder of the business had discovered himself. All that Samuel II could do after his father's death was follow his earlier advice, which was to trust the senior clerks to run Chiswell Street.

The Chiswell Street 'clerks' were extremely able men, with a vast experience of the industry. In yet another letter to his son, Whitbread senior had stressed their competence and, in particular, the importance of Maysey, Green, Yallowley and Sangster.

Mr Maysey there is no replacing of him. Mr Green or Mr Green & Son falling, the very Brewing is at an end. Mr Yallowly and Sangster are very important & the business of the Cash a thing of such Trust & Confidence, that cannot be placed in new people. Indeed I think it impossible even if I had my Health and spirits to carry it on myself if any of their lives should drop. Therefore I may truly say nobody else could.

What this encomium ignored was that the team was past its prime. By 1796, two had already died, Maysey in 1794 and Green the year after. And Green's deputy, David Jennings, was not in the same class – 'it is a matter of indifference if he continues or not,' Whitbread senior had judged.

This left Jacob Yallowley and Robert Sangster. They were, indeed, as professional and competent as Sam I had described them. But they shared one serious shortcoming; they had always been employees and not owners of the brewery. When it came to finance, that had always been the responsibility of their boss. And, as Sam II discovered with terrifying speed, brewing was an incredibly cash-hungry business.

All commercial activity in Georgian England was filled with uncertainties. England was at war for 63 years between 1695 and 1815, with alternating booms and slumps undermining even the soundest businesses. Brewing was no exception. The price of hops was particularly volatile and as production grew, so did Whitbread's exposure to sudden changes in the price of the commodities it used in brewing.

The time-lag between brewing and selling porter also imposed a severe strain on the brewery's cash flow. Another pressure was the growing support it was forced to give to publicans. By the turn of the century, Whitbread was selling beer to 600 pubs and owned the leases of something like 50. Publicans' outstanding debts approached £80,000. At the lowest point in the annual financial cycle, the brewery's need for cash could be as much as £200,000.

At the high point, of course, the cash pendulum swung the other way, with the surplus building up to substantial proportions. As well as sales, Whitbread's balances included money 'banked' with the brewery by a surprising number of people. One source was savings clubs run by publicans for their customers. By 1796 deposits from clubs totalled £9,530. Then there were funds belonging to employees and their relations. Broughton Maysey, for example, had had £5,000 on deposit with the brewery and in 1796 the staff's private accounts totalled £37,800. In periods of positive cash flow, Whitbread put these funds on deposit in the money market.

When cash was short, however, the deposits were used by the brewery. They were supplemented by loans from suppliers, in particular hop and malt factors, who were also good for credit in difficult times. But there were times when even greater backing was needed, and then Samuel I turned to his own network of friends and associates, such as the father of his first wife, William Hayton, and his lawyer and close neighbour, William Wilshere. If necessary, he used his estates as collateral, but such was his reputation that his note of hand was usually more than adequate. Shrewd and experienced, Whitbread senior manipulated the tidal flow of finance for his brewery with consummate skill.

His death left the business dreadfully exposed, especially as it coincided with the beginning of the war with Napoleon. Commercial panic swept through the country. Within weeks of Samuel I's death, the brewery was faced with a cash crisis.

The faithful clerks put their hands in their own pockets, which turned out to be surprisingly deep; Yallowley and Sangster between them lent the brewery £10,000 and Jennings cashed another £5,000 from the long annuities, although he insisted that he should receive the same return on the money and that enough capital should eventually be replaced in the annuities to restore their redemption value.

Samuel II raised a £13,000 mortgage, but much more was needed. So he turned to his own friends. James Brogden lent £11,490 in July 1796 and then the following February another £27,900 was paid into the brewery by a consortium including General Fitzpatrick, Lord Robert Spencer and Sir Culling Smith who, incidentally, bought Bedwell Park ten years later. Like

Robert Sangster aged 38, also painted by George Romney in 1787. Between them, Sangster and Yallowley ran the brewery for many years.

Late in 1795, Henry Holland was commissioned by Samuel II to rebuild his new home, Southill. Work began the following summer, and the project was completed in 1802 at a cost of £54,188 16s. 10d. The Building of Southill by George Garrard, 1803, is based on a watercolour sketch the artist had made of the reconstruction in progress in 1797.

WHITBREAD PUBS TODAY
St Paul's Tavern, on the corner
of Chiswell Street and Milton
Street. There has been a pub
on this site at least since 1826.
Some of Whitbread's offices
can be seen on the right of the
photograph *below*.

Jennings, all this money was taken out of immature investments, which
cost nearly twice as much to repay. Even the £5,200 that George Grey,
Samuel II's brother-in-law, lent in 1801, cost the brewery £8,700 to repay,
plus interest at more than 5 per cent.

Whitbread might have lent the brewery more himself, but he had
commissioned Henry Holland to redevelop Southill, which the famous
architect was doing regardless of expense. The result was, to quote Sir
Nikolaus Pevsner, 'one of the most exquisite English understatements', but
the improvements had cost its owner over £50,000.

Samuel II was also deeply embroiled in the settlement of his father's will,
which ran to 126 pages and involved bequests totalling an estimated
£124,000. As it had been made just less than a year before Samuel I's death,
his son might have challenged the will's validity. Instead he accepted
responsibility for discharging it in full. It turned out to be a mammoth task
which was still uncompleted at his own death, as well as imposing a huge
drain on his finances.

A solution had to be found. Short of selling the business as a whole, a
prospect even less likely in such deeply uncertain and depressed times than
when Sam I had been trying, Whitbread could only see one answer, even
though his father had forecast that it would result in ruin. Partners.

Yallowley and Sangster agreed to take up a ninth share each. This did
nothing to ease his own financial position, as he had to lend them the
money to buy their shares. For a cash infusion into the brewery, Whitbread
turned to the radical merchant banker Timothy 'Equality' Brown, who
advanced £100,000 in return for a one-third share in the business. He also,

Sir IOHN BARLEYCORN — MISS HOP — (and their only child) MASTER PORTER
Dedicated to the Publicans of London Pub. by Tho. Tegg ...

Sir John Barleycorn, Miss Hop (and their only child) Master Porter. *This engraving, illustrating the close relationship between agriculture and beer, was published by Thomas Tegg c.1800.*

of course, brought the implicit promise of short-term funding from his bank, or so the brewery assumed.

Whitbread's fund-raising enabled the brewery to maintain production for the next three years, but then hop and malt prices jumped violently at the same time as the Government raised the rate of duty. In November 1799, for the first time for nearly 40 years, the price of porter went up from 30s. to 35s. a barrel.

The brewery could only respond by cutting back purchases of raw materials and production fell by a third to 137,000 barrels, the lowest level for 15 years. A furious Jennings resigned 'in a very unhandsome manner', to be replaced by Samuel Green junior, who turned out to be grossly incompetent and was fired two years later.

By this time Whitbread had persuaded his cousin Jacob Whitbread and his close parliamentary friend Benjamin Hobhouse to buy half his remaining shares in Chiswell Street, while Brown had passed one of his three-ninths on to his associate Joseph Godman. A year later Samuel sold a tenth of his remaining stake to William Wilshere, who was advising him about his father's will and who later built up his own investment in the brewery to a full share. But this still left Samuel as the largest shareholder, as Jacob Yallowley died and he had had to buy back his holding.

In theory, Samuel II was a sleeping partner and there was a clause in the partnership agreement which made it clear he was not expected to take an active role at Chiswell Street. He was, after all, by now an influential politician on the verge of office in the new Whig Government led by Charles James Fox. Whitbread had rather gracelessly insisted on taking his father's place as MP for Bedford Town in 1790. Samuel I's acquiescence was all the more extraordinary in view of the fact that his son was standing for the opposition. It took the elder Whitbread a year to get back into the

Joseph Godman senior became a partner in the brewery in 1799. Members of his family remained partners in Whitbread until it became a limited company 90 years later and are still shareholders.

Whitbread's Intire *engraving, published in 1795 by H. Humphrey, depicts Samuel II's speeches as an embarrassment to his Whig colleagues. As a beer barrel full of froth, he is made to look ridiculous while discussing his main concerns of 'Reform, Peace, Liberty, Equality, no Slave Trade, Peace' in Parliament.*

House of Commons as MP for Steyning in Sussex, which he represented until his death. If nothing else, it gave him the dubious pleasure of listening at first hand to his son's savagely outspoken attacks on his own party.

Samuel II's political career had begun in flamboyant fashion. He made an early reputation with a sarcastic speech opposing British interference in Catherine the Great's aggressive attitude to Turkey. Five years later, in 1797, he moved an ill-timed motion of censure against the Tory Prime Minister, William Pitt, for his handling of the mutiny at Spithead. And he had begun a career-long campaign in support of the poor, whose plight in the 1790s was appalling, particularly in the country, where many were in danger of starvation owing to war prices and low wages. When Pitt fell from office in 1801, after nearly 20 years in power, Whitbread was almost justified in expecting a junior minister's post in the new government. He didn't get one, but if anything that merely heightened the intensity of his political activities.

That didn't save him from involvement in the affairs of Chiswell Street.

The fly in the ointment was Timothy Brown. As early as 1802 Brown was writing to Whitbread to complain about the way Sangster and Yallowley were limiting allowances to certain employees. Brown's real complaint, however, was that the brewery was not depositing its money in his bank. 'I have it loudly hinted how little influence I had in the Brewery that it was my Money only was wanted and now I feel it.'

Four years later the row was still rumbling on. It came to a head in October 1806 when Whitbread wrote to the postal authorities instructing them not to deliver any brewery mail addressed to Brown to his Lombard Street office, but to take it direct to Chiswell Street. Brown was outraged. The action, he wrote angrily to Whitbread on 20 October, was as good as 'stamping my character as unfit to be trusted . . . I feel as low as you would intend, lower than any Partner or Letter Carrier.' And he threatened to resign. 'Let me have my money and such portion as is my due.'

Three years later, however, he was still a partner and in rather different trouble, with his own bank's finances – as Benjamin Hobhouse explained to him delicately – rumoured to be 'subject to some inconvenience in consequence of an unexpected pressure of demand upon it'. This time it was the brewery that wanted to end the association. Hastily, Brown wrote back: 'My dear Sir, There was a time when I would have taken my capital out of the concern in Chiswell Street and retired; that time is past and however great the reluctance may be in any or all of the partners to inform me my continuance is not agreeable, my explicit answer to the proposition made is NO.'

Six months later Brown was still refusing to agree a settlement and it wasn't until August 1810, after an independent arbitrator had been called in to revalue the Rest, the annual midsummer valuation of the brewery's assets, that he finally agreed a figure. Even then he was holding out for better terms, but luckily another run on his bank occurred. 'We paid him £50,000 before 3 o'clock the next day and he is entirely gone,' Whitbread wrote relievedly to Lord Grey on 3 August. He added: 'Thank you for your kind expressions respecting my concerns. There are reasons why I should like if it were possible to discharge my mind of all concerns in trade. The riddance of Brown has taken away one very material one, but with so large a stake and so much depending on my name and continuance, it is very difficult. There are temptations of interest, too, and the management exceedingly easy.'

Whitbread had, it appeared, acquired a knowledge of and an attachment to the family business which he would not have admitted 15 years earlier. But he was just as much an absentee proprietor, even if his shareholding had climbed back to 33 per cent.

And to claim that the management was easy was a gross injustice to the man who had been holding the brewery together. The last of the faithful clerks, Robert Sangster had been quietly keeping Chiswell Street in business throughout some of the most difficult years the industry had ever experienced. Hop prices had fallen from the extreme heights they had reached at the turn of the century, but both malt and hops were still much more expensive than in the past. Worse, they continued to move up and down, forcing frequent changes in the price of beer, which fluctuated from 35s. to 55s. a barrel in a way guaranteed to outrage consumers.

Under the pressure of increased raw material costs, Sangster had reduced Chiswell Street's annual production to just over 100,000 barrels from 1804 onwards. It was no more than half its capacity, but thanks to the higher wholesale price and the reduced burden of financing implicit in brewing less beer, average profits were not far off the record years of the 1790s.

But Sangster was growing old. By 1810 he had been working for the Whitbreads, man and boy, for 46 years. He had started work the year Samuel II was born. He had done well and Whitbread senior had been

A bust of Timothy Brown, the famous 'Equality' Brown, presented by a descendant to Whitbread in 1977.

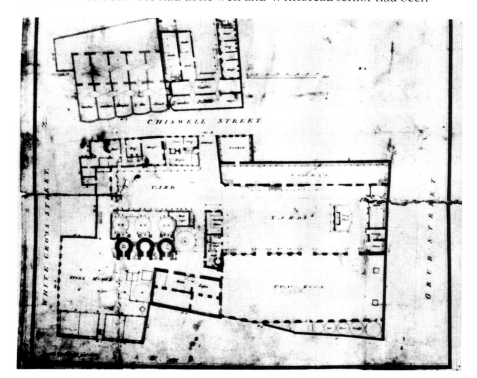

A plan showing the extent of the brewery in 1800, by which time it had expanded to both sides of Chiswell Street.

John Martineau became a partner in the brewery in 1812. His descendants have been partners and subsequently shareholders in Whitbread ever since.

generous, paying him handsome bonuses and making sure he had the opportunity to become a partner after his death. He had already paid off his debt to the brewery and was again banking surplus funds in its accounts. For the previous eight years he had effectively been in sole charge of Chiswell Street. The other partners had been men like Timothy Brown, only interested in how much the brewery was going to be able to pay them each year. Sangster did not blame them. He had learned to understand the mentality of the rich, and even differentiate between the greed of bankers and the dispassionate determination of the landed gentry to protect their capital.

But he couldn't help worrying about the future of the brewery which he had done so much to help create and which, in spite of running at half speed, was still the greatest in London. None of the other partners had the faintest idea about how to run Chiswell Street. So he quietly set out to look for a successor. He found him in John Martineau, the senior partner in a medium-sized brewery on the Thames at Lambeth.

The Martineaus came from a Norfolk banking family but had been brewing in London since 1783. The brewery was smaller than Whitbread's but it owned 38 public houses and had its own maltings in Norfolk. Since 1808 there had been three partners, Martineau, his son Joseph, and Michael Bland, who was also from a Norfolk banking background. Most importantly, though, John Martineau was a first-rate brewer. He was a well-known figure within the trade and had been its spokesman before several parliamentary committees.

He had also been the arbitrator in the dispute over the valuation of the 1810 Rest. Sangster had been impressed by Martineau's judgement and had made further enquiries. A year later, he persuaded Samuel II to begin negotiations for a merger of the two breweries. 'M and his two sons will

The Triumph of Quassia, published by H. Humphrey in 1806, depicts the main brewers of the time carrying Quassi, a negro who, in 1730, discovered medicinal properties in a South American tree now named after him. Bitter in taste, quassia was used by brewers during the Napoleonic wars as a substitute for high-priced hops. Sam II is at the front of the barrel, Combe at the back, followed by Barclay in the blue coat. On the horse are Lord W. Pelty, Lord Grenville and Charles James Fox.

MANAGEMENT – or – BUTTS & HOGSHEADS.

bring about one-sixth part of the Trade to yourself and four in point of number of persons,' he reported to Whitbread, adding: 'the disproportion is great, but perhaps in the present instance that is of small consequence when it is considered that it is young blood that they bring into the Concern.'

It took a year to complete the deal, but the two businesses came together in the summer of 1812. The Martineau brewery was closed and Chiswell Street began supplying the 38 tied houses and 50 free houses that had been its customers. The Whitbread partners had £300,000 of the nominal capital, with the three new managing partners putting up £25,000 each. They each received a salary of £500 a year, as did Sangster.

From Whitbread's point of view, the merger had come none too soon. He was not yet 50, but he was beginning to suffer from ill health. From 1809 he was affected by what he described as listlessness and dejection. He had given up riding to hounds a few years earlier, partly because his wife, Lady Elizabeth, disliked it, and since then he had put on a great deal of weight. A letter from his doctor in August 1810 advised him to be careful not to eat or drink too much and warned that apoplexy most commonly occurred in bulky people. He also recommended bleeding from the nape of the neck to relieve the headaches that were starting to plague his patient.

Two years later Whitbread's friend Thomas Creevey, who was staying at Southill, wrote to his wife 'there is some unfortunate defect in his constitution, his tendency to manufacture blood and fat is beyond everything I ever heard of . . . I was struck beyond measure just now at the prodigious Gills and Collops in his neck.'

George Cruikshank's Management – or – Butts & Hogsheads *(1812) is a satirical look at the new Drury Lane Theatre under Whitbread's management. Samuel II stirs 'expectations' and other papers into the vat, while 'John Bull' (the subscribers) sits by the tap, waiting in vain for 'profits' to appear. These are intercepted by Richard and Tom Sheridan (they were due compensation for their stake in the old theatre company).*

Lady Elizabeth Whitbread, who married Samuel II in 1788.

Administring (sic) to an Old Friend!! Or the rapid effects of Whitbread's Intire is one of a series of cartoons published in 1805 and 1806 on the impeachment proceedings against Viscount Melville. Most had the common theme that, through being forced to drink too much of Whitbread's porter, Melville would vomit up the money he had embezzled from the Navy.

Whitbread was also becoming increasingly unhappy about his political career. He had acquired a national reputation in 1806 when he had impeached Lord Melville for misuse of public money while Treasurer of the Navy. But although the Whigs had regained power no place was found for Whitbread in the government. One of the reasons was snobbery. Although brewing was one of the more respectable trades, it was still trade. But the other was more profound. He was an uncomfortable person. In the House his speeches were too sincere and too intemperate. Outside it he was too outspoken and too independent of the party line. He advocated reform of the Poor Law, struggled for the establishment of schools and was a consistent opponent of war. He had an embarrassing habit of going too far in his attacks on individuals, and a self-destructive tendency to pick the wrong ones to attack. Wellington, for example, was a frequent target.

As time went by he became more and more upset at being bypassed for office. It drove him to further extremes of political behaviour, and reduced his chances even more.

He consoled himself with a variety of activities, of which the most quixotic was his involvement in the Drury Lane Theatre. In 1809 the theatre was destroyed by fire, by which time its debts were already almost half a million pounds. Whitbread chaired the committee formed to rebuild it and, as well as involving himself in a public subscription which raised £300,000, persuaded many of his friends and employees to take up £100 shares in the new theatre. It was built with remarkable speed, reopening on 10 October 1812, but that was only the beginning of the hard struggle to make it pay. Whitbread's son-in-law, Captain William Waldegrave, wrote later that the Drury Lane Theatre probably contributed more than any other business to 'perplex, worry and fatigue a mind already more than sufficiently engaged'.

In the last few months of his life, Whitbread lost his normal exuberance. His family and friends lived in daily fear of what the medical profession at the time described as an apoplexy or a paralytic seizure. He began to worry obsessively about money, although the rise in the value of land meant he was actually richer than ever.

In the middle of June 1815 he admitted to being oppressed with an intolerable headache. A fortnight later there was a disturbance among the footmen at the door of the Vauxhall pleasure gardens as he was leaving. He is reported to have turned to his wife and said wildly: 'They are hissing me. I am become an object of universal abhorrence.' The following Tuesday, however, he spoke in the House of Commons more in his usual style. But the next day, after a meeting at Drury Lane, he told Henry Holland's son Lancelot, with whom he was walking down Piccadilly: 'The world will point and scoff at me. The populace will pull down my house.' The next morning he cut his throat with a razor.

Henry Weekes's monument to Sam II and his wife in St Mary's Church, Cardington, sculptured in 1849, shows them clasped together in prayer.

The village of Cardington in Bedfordshire has close connections with the Whitbread family. Samuel I bought his first land here 'because it was the place of my birth and inheritance of my Father's.'

The Sherlock Holmes Tavern in London
became a Whitbread pub in 1951, although
there has been a pub on this site for 200
years or more. Before 1953 it was the
Northumberland Arms Hotel, a popular haunt
of Sir Arthur Conan Doyle and mentioned in
his books as a meeting-place for Holmes
and Dr Watson.

CHAPTER FOUR

A PUBLIC BENEFIT

1815–1834

For most people in the United Kingdom, 1815 was a time to celebrate, for had not the man who had straddled Europe for a generation, the Emperor of the French, Napoleon Buonaparte, the dreaded 'Boney' himself, finally met his Waterloo at the hands of that great Englishman, the Duke of Wellington? Peace at last!

And at last the opportunity to address some of the problems at home, of which there were all too many.

For a start, something like one in five people were so poorly paid, if at all, that they had to have their wages supplemented from parish rates. Many labourers in the countryside were paupers even when they were in full work. And their plight had been worsened by the high cost of wheat, which had risen from 43s. a quarter in 1793, the year before war broke out, to 126s. a quarter in 1812.

It was unfortunate, too, that the war had coincided with the early years of the Industrial Revolution. To quote G. M. Trevelyan: 'A rampant individualism, inspired by no idea beyond quick money returns, set up the cheap and nasty model of modern industrial life and its surroundings. Town planning, sanitation and amenity were things undreamt of by the vulgarian makers of the new world, while the aristocratic ruling class enjoyed its own pleasant life apart.'

Worse still, the price of beer had gone up!

The big brewers had been under attack for profiteering and monopoly ever since they raised the price of beer from 30s. to 35s. a barrel at the end of 1799. There was just enough truth in the charges to put them on the defensive. The most powerful members of the Brewers' Company had, it was true, formed themselves into a Committee of Porter Brewers as far back as 1795, with the object of regulating price changes. They had collectively bought Continental barley. It was Timothy Brown who explained to the

The Bull and Last, Kentish Town, in 1820. Coaching inns were built all around the edge of London on the main routes into the capital. As the population of the capital expanded during the nineteenth century, more and more Londoners walked out for pleasure to pubs like this – which was good for their trade and for the the city's breweries.

Bank of England that the 'conspiracy' was only an attempt to lower the price 'for a public Benefit'. They had, on occasion, appeared slow to drop their prices following falls in their costs, although they argued that this was only because they were restoring the strength of their beer, itself an implicit admission that it had been weakened in the first place. And they had, undeniably, hugely increased their ties with public houses since the turn of the century. By 1810 close to 80 per cent of all London pubs were tied to one or other of the big porter brewers, either through loans or leases. At Whitbread the figure was 82 per cent.

The fact that this last situation had been imposed on them by the financial plight of publicans and that it was costing them a fortune – in Whitbread's case more than £100,000 in 1810, equal to a £1 discount on every barrel sold to a tied house – made little impression on their critics. Nor did they accept that the rises in the price of beer were due to higher costs. Some critics were so convinced that the big brewers were profiteering when the price of beer rose to 5*d.* a quart in August 1803 that they launched their own brewery in competition, with the backing of a group of dissatisfied publicans. To the embarrassment of the existing industry, the Genuine Beer Brewery in Golden Lane initially proved a great success and its rivals were far from unhappy when an over-generous dividend policy undermined its competitiveness.

The pressure on margins was at its worst in 1812, the year that Whitbread and Martineau merged. Two bad grain harvests had exhausted brewers' stocks and malt prices were at record levels. The only alternative to an increase in the price of beer was the use of duty-free sugar, great stocks of which were awaiting export in bonded warehouses. Samuel Whitbread pleaded the brewers' case with the Chancellor of the Exchequer, Nicholas Vansittart, but to no avail. The following January beer was up 20 per cent in price at 6*d.* a quart.

Five years later the industry was under attack again, this time from John Beaumont, a builder who was also a Westminster JP. Beaumont had built 150 houses 'on spec' in Stepney and Shepherd's Bush, with a 'superior public house on each estate for the necessary convenience of tenants'. When he was refused licences for his new pubs, he whipped up an anti-monopoly movement that inspired a parliamentary inquiry in 1818. Eleven leading brewers, including John Martineau, were quizzed by the Select Committee. It exonerated them on price, profit and quality and decided that there were still just enough free houses to ensure competition between porter brewers.

Martineau's inclusion was one measure of the success of his merger with Whitbread. Another was the way in which Chiswell Street had recovered its momentum. It had taken the new managing partners only three years to lift output above 160,000 barrels and, although bad harvests had cut that back in the previous couple of years, the upward trend was set to resume.

Behind the revival was a tremendous effort to bring the brewery up to date. A visitor whom John Martineau walked round the brewery in October 1818 recorded that

Since the last time I saw this concern they have fitted up their great Store House with Vessels (Rounds) of 10 Bls each for cleansing, with very complete apparatus attached. They have three complete sets, for 3 Brewings, and it is altogether an immense thing, the most extensive and complete in its kind anywhere to be seen.

Taking a glass of ale outside an inn (from Revd Isaac Taylor's Scenes of British Wealth, *London, 1823). While some London pubs remained free houses, four-fifths were already tied to the capital's breweries by tenancies or loans.*

The Genuine Beer Brewery, Golden Lane, in 1807. The brewery was established about half a mile away from Chiswell Street in 1804 with the backing of publicans who objected to the high price existing breweries were charging for beer. Initially successful, it was brought down by an over-generous dividend policy.

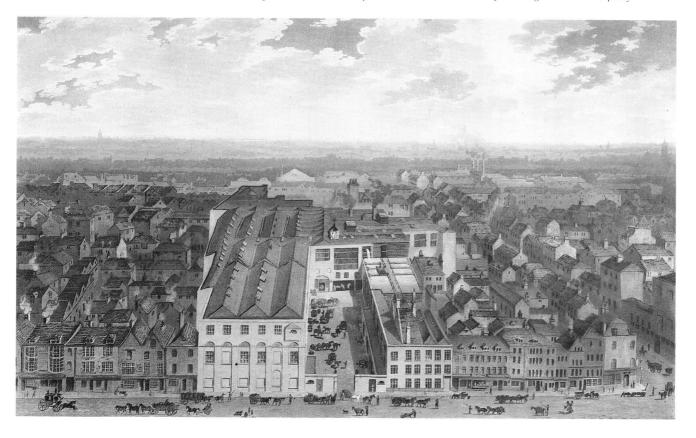

They wash out all the Vessels every time they are used by men going in. Their Squares are fixed at the upper end of their great house and command all the Cleansing Rounds.

The Coolers are high above the Squares and the Worts are refrigerated by running from the Coolers thro a pipe placed within a larger one and with a smaller passing within itself – thro the outer and inner pipe a stream of water is forced by the Liquor Pumps and so up to the liquor Back, and the Worts thus pass between two columns of Water and are cooled to any degree the Brewer pleases. A Thermometer is immersed in the Worts pipe near the Squares through a Stuffing Box and so continues fixed; by which the temperature is ascertained easily and completely – and is regulated in increasing or lessening the supply of worts from the Cooler, by a stop cock.

The visitor noticed large copper pipes coiling round a brick cistern. Martineau explained that this was filled from the brewery's well and that passing new beer through the pipes in the hot summer months cooled it to the same temperature as the water, about 55°F. The well was 120 feet deep and the water was 'peculiarly pellucid and the supply inexhaustible'.

Another change was abandoning the use of coppers. Instead,

They Boil their Worts in their Cast Iron Hop Back, by means of steam pipes continued twice round it in the inside near the bottom. They have covered over their Hop Back with a wooden cover or roof lined inside with thin Copper. They have 4 sheet iron boilers for raising steam for this purpose and Mr Martineau confessed that there is no saving of coal, but says the Boiling is most completely effected, that the cooperation or reducing is quicker, the flavour is improved and all the labour of returning the Hops is saved. I saw by a thermometer fixed into the steam pipes that the heat was up to 280 degrees.

Financing the recovery had not been easy. To begin with, Samuel Whitbread's suicide had left a huge financial mess.

It is a measure of how much Samuel II had embroiled himself financially that he left the whole of his partnership in the brewery, which in 1812 had

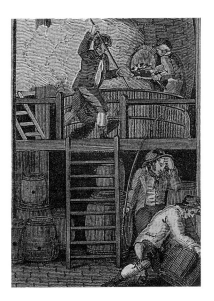

The Brewer (from The Book of English Trades, *London, 1821). While the big copper is being stoked, the mash-tun is stirred.*

Below, left and right: These sections through a porter brewery were taken from drawings of Chiswell Street by John Farey and published in 1815. Left: The Boulton & Watt steam engine on the left powers the whole process, but the horse mill can still be seen under the malt lofts. Right: This section through the Porter Tun-Room shows the mash-tuns and, below them, Samuel Whitbread's stone cisterns that had been made waterproof with such difficulty.

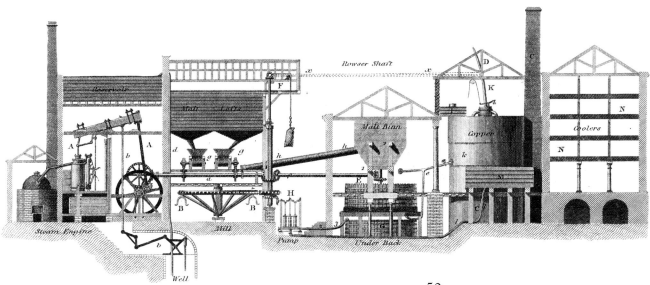

been worth £112,500, to Robert Sangster and William Wilshere to cover his debts. Wilshere was the largest creditor at just over £42,000 and Sangster the next at £20,000. Several more were owed £10,000 each, including his son-in-law, William, who had by this time become Lord Waldegrave. In addition, there was still a considerable amount owing to beneficiaries of his father's will. Altogether his debts totalled at least £200,000. Although the family's estates were largely unencumbered, all that was left of its investment in the brewery was ownership of the premises in Chiswell Street, valued at £45,000.

Samuel II had made Wilshere and Sangster his executors, but in 1816 they handed this responsibility over to Whitbread's elder son William Henry on 5 March, his 21st birthday. It took him three years to sort out his father's tangled affairs, but then he sold the freeholds and leaseholds of the premises to the brewery in return for a partnership. Two years later his younger brother also became a partner.

Why they decided to continue the family tradition was never stated. They were never involved in the management of Chiswell Street. Thanks to the patronage of the Duke of Bedford, William had already taken his father's place as MP for Bedford, a seat he held until 1834, and his brother was to be the member for Middlesex from 1820 to 1830. It is probable the reason was simply that a partnership in the brewery looked the most profitable way to get a return on the capital they had locked up in it.

Replacing Samuel II's investment in the brewery was only one of the problems the new managers faced. Although malt prices had fallen from their peak, they were still twice their pre-war average. The need to restock meant that Whitbread had £79,000 tied up in malt by 1816. A year later the hop harvest failed and the price of hops doubled and then tripled, requiring another £15,000. On the plus side, malt supplies were at least guaranteed from the Martineau maltings in Norfolk, worth £18,800 when they were valued in 1826. By then Whitbread Martineau & Co., as the partnership was now called, had acquired a large wharf and malt store at the western end of the City Road basin of the Lea Union Canal, which had just linked the Regent's Park Canal to the Lea Navigation at Bethnal Green.

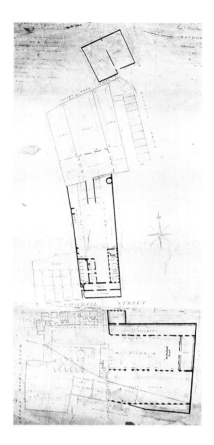

By 1817, the Chiswell Street brewery had expanded even further, although it did not reach its maximum extent for another 70 years.

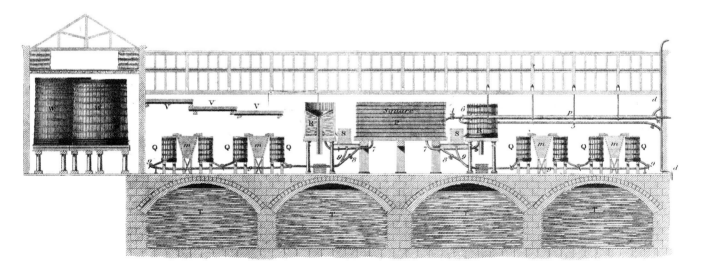

WHITBREAD PUBS TODAY

The Ship Anson, on The Hard in
Portsmouth, was listed in local
directories as a pub in 1784. The
mock-Tudor front was added in 1923.
The Ship Anson has been a Whitbread
pub since the takeover of Brickwoods'
brewery in 1971. In a recent
refurbishment, the pub was extended
to take in what was previously a
separate pub next door on the left.

The Brewery (from Revd Isaac Taylor's Scenes of British Wealth, London, 1823). Here, the mash-tuns are being stirred.

By then, too, John Martineau and his son had completed their revitalization of Chiswell Street and had crowned their programme with a new record of 213,000 barrels in 1823. This still left Whitbread narrowly behind Truman and a long way from the industry leader, Thrale Barclay Perkins, which was up to 350,000 barrels. But it was a classic example of the benefits of 'hands-on' management and a triumphant vindication of the merger for the aged Robert Sangster, who had retired in 1815 after an unbeaten 50 years.

Thomas Creevey was a guest at the brewery in May 1823. 'We sat down 22, I think. The entertainment of the day to me was going over the Brewery after dinner by gaslight. A stable, brilliantly illuminated, containing ninety horses worth 50 or 60 guineas apiece upon an average, is a sight to be seen nowhere but in this tight little island. The beauty and amiability of the horses was quite affecting; such as were lying down we favoured with sitting upon – four or five of us upon a horse.'

The year was, though the brewers did not know it, an all-time peak for porter, with a total for London of 1.8 million barrels, the culmination of a rising trend that had lasted for 50 years. Within seven years, output would be down by more than 20 per cent.

The reason was not the continuing assault on the monopoly that the Common Brewers were assumed to enjoy because of their control of so many pubs. This was strong enough to persuade the Government to pass the Intermediate Beer Act the same year. The Act halved the rate of duty paid on porter to 5s. a barrel for a weaker beer which could only be made by 'intermediate' breweries. These had to have no connection with existing breweries or maltings, could only sell to free houses, and had their prices firmly fixed. Perhaps not surprisingly, they were not a success. An Act the following year to encourage small retail breweries selling their production from their own premises was equally ineffectual as a challenge to the monopoly of the big brewers.

Whitbread's Wharf, painted by George Garrard in 1796, on the south side of the Thames near London Bridge. Whitbread's main wharf was on the north side of the river, near Blackfriars Bridge.

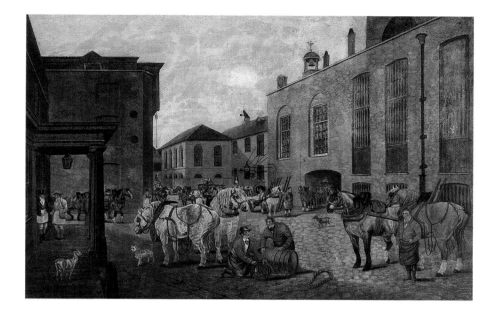

View of the South Yard at Chiswell Street, painted by D. Wolstenholme junior in 1820. In the centre is the Sugar Room, with the Porter Tun-Room to its right. The archway on the left is the entrance to the Partners' House. The brewery is on the right.

What did hit the big houses was a 40 per cent reduction in the duty on spirits to 7s. a gallon in 1825. The effect was catastrophic. Within one year England's gin consumption had doubled to 7.4 million gallons. And sales of beer slumped.

Once again the forces of moderation allied in favour of good, healthy British beer against the demon gin. Thomas Creevey's friend the Reverend Sydney Smith, an irrepressible wit who had nicknamed Samuel Whitbread II 'the Great Fermentator' in a pun on his trade and his pugnacious politics, was only one of the influential voices calling for action. 'What two ideas are more inseparable than Beer and Britannia?' he trumpeted in the *Edinburgh Review*, the influential monthly magazine that he had founded.

The first move, Thomas Estcourt's Licensing Bill, gave publicans the right to appeal if a licence was refused or withdrawn. This was more a belated strike against the brewers' monopoly, however, and had no effect on gin sales. Two years later, in April 1830, in a desperate attempt to win popularity in the face of mounting criticism, the Tory Government called a new enquiry, took evidence for a fortnight, and passed what became known as the Duke of Wellington's Beer House Act 'to permit the general sale of beer and cider by retail'. Any householder liable for the Poor Rate could obtain a licence to sell beer from his home or shop on payment of two guineas a year.

This was not a solution Martineau and his cronies on the Committee of Porter Brewers approved at all. They were in favour of a reduction in the duty on beer, but to allow everyone to sell it was a disaster, not so much for themselves but for their customers and debtors, the publicans. Charles Barclay told the House of Commons enquiry: 'It would change the beer trade from victuallers to chandlers, those who would adulterate it and spoil it, and instead of having any benefit from it, the country gentlemen would soon be up in arms by having beer shops and beer houses established in every part of their country.' And Charles Calvert forecast it would prove 'an

These pages:
Draymen and drays were the only means of transporting beer barrels to the pubs until motorized transport arrived in the twentieth century. As such, they were a prominent feature of everyday life, making regular deliveries to pubs.

Act for the increase of drunkenness and the consumption of smuggled spirits'.

Their prophesies were utterly correct. Between October, when the law came into force, and the end of the year, 24,000 licences were taken out. In Liverpool the rate was 50 new beerhouses a day. Within months drinking dens with mud walls and cellars were springing up on the edges of villages all over the country. Riotous behaviour and illegal spirit drinking were the predictable and uncontrollable consequences. Over the next ten years the quantity of malt used for brewing rose by 28 per cent but consumption of British gin increased by a third.

The impact on the existing licensed victuallers was as devastating as the brewers had forecast. Hundreds went bankrupt. The knock-on effect on their major creditors was almost as bad. Whitbread alone was forced to write its capital down by £67,500 to £382,500 in 1830 due to 'bad and desperate debts', as well as recording an annual loss of £5,000, the first in its history. Outstanding loans to publicans were up to £316,000, equal to £2.14s. for every barrel the brewery produced in the year. By 1830 Whitbread was supplying 670 public houses. This was more than twice as many as 20 years earlier, when 82 per cent had been tied. Now, ironically, the 'tie' was down to 65 per cent, with the number of free houses supplied up more than fourfold. Whitbread was, in fact, struggling to reduce its links with publicans as fast as it could, not for any ideological reason but because they were proving painfully uneconomic.

Within three years, another Select Committee was sitting to 'inquire into the extent, causes and consequences of the prevailing vice of intoxication among the labouring classes of the United Kingdom'. It summarized its findings as follows:

1: Extent of Evil. Decline among higher and middle classes. Increase among labouring classes.
2: Remote causes. Former example of upper classes. Continuance of ancient convivial customs in connection with important events in life and with commercial transactions.
3: Immediate causes. Increased number of places where intoxicating drinks are sold, average one to 20 families.
4: Consequences to individual character. Destruction of: Health and Mental capacity and vigour. Irritation of worst passions. Extinction of moral and religious principles.
5: Consequences to National welfare. Waste of grain by conversion of nutritious food into poison. Loss of productive labour, averaging one day in six. Loss of property at sea, through avoidable accidents. Comparative inefficiency of Army and Navy. Injury to national reputation abroad, through behaviour of seamen in foreign ports. Retardation of improvement. Increase of pauperism. Spread of crime.

And it suggested nearly a score of changes, including annual licensing by magistrates, restricted opening on Sundays and an end to the payment of wages in public houses. However, the Beerhouse Act that followed merely

distinguished between 'on' and 'off' sales, raising the cost of the licence to serve beer for consumption on the premises to three guineas and reducing the cost of an off-licence to one guinea.

It was in these unhappy and straitened circumstances that 75-year-old John Martineau took a tasting pipe and began his regular Friday afternoon inspection of the Chiswell Street vats. He had had a 'severe paralytic and apoplectic attack' a few years earlier which had left him prone to violent pains in the head. Although he had recovered his mobility, his partners had arranged for him to be accompanied around the brewery by a junior employee. This Friday, however, 4 April 1834, three weeks before his seventy-sixth birthday, Martineau dismissed his minder and insisted on carrying out his inspection alone.

About five o'clock one of Chiswell Street's overseers went into the vat room and climbed up the ladder placed against one of them. He found Martineau inside, face down in about two feet of beer. 'An alarm was instantly given and medical assistance promptly arrived, but the vital spark was extinct.' At the inquest the next day, the medical opinion was that the deceased had been suddenly seized with apoplexy and had fallen into the vat, and the jury returned the verdict: 'Died by the Visitation of God.'

The Old Vat House in Chiswell Street,
painted in 1873. The vats varied between 24 ft
and 38 ft in height, and each contained
2,000–3,000 barrels.

CHAPTER FIVE

THE QUESTION AT ISSUE

1834–1889

On the morning of 26 July 1866 the partners in the Whitbread brewery gathered in Chiswell Street for a special meeting. They spanned two generations. The older was represented by William Henry and Samuel Charles Whitbread, John Manning-Needham, Lord Broughton, Joseph Godman and Philip Worsley. Manning-Needham had been a partner since 1837. Broughton and Godman were respectively the sons of Benjamin Hobhouse and Joseph Godman senior, who had been two of the earliest investors to come to the rescue of Samuel II. And Philip Worsley was another Sangster, an indispensable clerk who had been rewarded with a partnership.

The younger included Godman's sons Richard and Frederick, Manning-Needham's son Francis, Worsley's son Richard and John Martineau's grandson, another John. The last two had just joined and Francis had only been a partner for three years.

The older men were dressed in heavily braided black frock-coats and tight black trousers, with white chokers and white stockings showing above their low shoes. The younger generation's clothing was only marginally less sombre. It was, after all, only five years since Prince Albert's death. Fortunately the Palace was still a customer for Whitbread's porter.

As the senior partner, William Whitbread opened the proceedings. He had been asked, he said, to present an open letter. It read as follows:

As there now exists some difference of opinion among the Managing Partners as to the course to be followed for the future, it seems desirable to take the opinion of all the partners as to the course to be pursued. The question at issue is in fact this, whether we should continue the practice of the last few years and extend our trade, or whether we should return to the practice of many years previous and confine our transactions to much smaller limits.

Joseph Martineau became a managing partner in Whitbread with his father, John, in 1812.

The reader paused. Some partners glanced at their neighbours, others scrupulously avoided catching anyone's eyes. They all knew exactly who had written the letter and at whom it was aimed. He continued:

'Before coming to any conclusion upon this point, it will be desirable to trace the effects of the different courses upon the profits of the business.'

The letter proceeded to summarize the brewery's trade since 1832, when the number of London pubs served by the brewery had been 769. Four years later it had crept up to 781, but since then it had slowly but steadily declined until 1862, when it had fallen to 562, 'in other words, a loss of considerably more than one-fourth of the customers and this too at a time when the population of London was increasing at an incredible rate'.

A good point. The whole of the country, for that matter, was experiencing a population explosion. Between 1801 and 1851, the number of people living in England and Wales had doubled from 9 million to 18 million. Fifteen years later it was nearly 21 million.

The reason for the growth was better health and lower mortality rates, especially among the young. The turning-point had been 1830, when the July Revolution in Paris had sparked the Farm Labourers' Rising, which coincided with the arrival of cholera in London. Lord Grey's Reform Act two years later was followed by a new Poor Law and a period of quiet prosperity which ended in a glorious harvest in 1835. Recession was quick to follow. Three years later the harvest failed, gold had to be exported to pay for food and the Bank of England was only saved by credits from Paris and Hamburg. Poverty and unemployment became rife. Wages fell by more than 60 per cent in the industrial North, where the average income was something like 1s. 6d. a week.

The Chartists called for revolution. The Free Trade League demanded a less radical but equally fundamental change. The politicians responded with a combination of repression and reform. Luckily, reform predominated. The

The Eagle Tavern in Islington, north London, with its grand façade that dominated the surrounding buildings. Built in 1839–40, its inspiration – as of many other pubs of the time – was nineteenth-century neo-classicism. The Eagle's patrons enjoyed pleasure grounds with singing and dancing and a famous Grecian saloon. The pub was demolished in 1899.

Factory Inspectors of 1834 were followed by Prison Inspectors, School Inspectors, Railway Inspectors and Mines Inspectors. Jeremy Bentham's concept of a trained Civil Service was given impetus by Edwin Chadwick's cadre of Assistant Commissioners, who toured the country gathering data, sometimes in the face of violence. When they appeared in Todmorden, the industrialist John Fielden rang his factory bells and beat them out of town. Once they had to be protected by cavalry. The birth of the English Civil Servant was a dramatic affair.

Their activities were part of the start of a Public Welfare Service. The pivotal year was 1846, which saw the Factory Act, the Education Minute and the Baths and Washhouses Act, the first of a string of public health laws which ended with the Burials Act six years later. Peel repealed the Corn Laws that same year, stimulating an immediate crash followed by an economic boom.

The men gathered in the Partner's Room in Chiswell Street were the beneficiaries of this golden era, opened as it seemed in retrospect by the Great Exhibition 15 years earlier. But the amazing growth of the economy seemed to be passing them by. As the open letter disclosed, the trade in porter had fallen from 187,000 barrels in 1832 to 127,000 barrels in 1862, a drop over the 30 years of 60,000 barrels. This had been partly offset by the decision, taken in 1834, to start brewing a mild ale in response to growing public preference for less alcoholic beers. Demand for Whitbread's new 'stout' had grown to 40,000 barrels, but this still left a shortfall of 20,000 barrels. And the writer of the letter was of the opinion that the ale business might have been in addition to the porter trade instead of a partial substitute for it.

In tracing the course of the profits throughout the period, however, government contracts had to be taken into account. Whitbread had been winning orders for beer from the Navy for a hundred years, but they had only become important since Victoria had ascended the throne. Having so many partners in Parliament was perhaps paying off at last. In many years contracts had more than made up for the fall in volume of 'regular' trade and they had in almost every instance been profitable. The only trouble was that they could not be relied on and occasionally fell into other hands. 'Viz the years ending Midsummer 1856 and 1861, in the former of which the profit was £7,103 and in the latter £10,470.'

But since 1862 the situation had changed. 'For the last four years, we have very considerably increased our town trade and the effect of this increase is shown by the profit which averaged £58,222 and is most conspicuously shown by the present year when the profit amounts to £60,822 without having obtained any contract whatever.'

The mood of the partners lightened. It seemed that the business was in good shape. And this in spite of the continuing hassle about the evils of drink from Dr Dawson Wade and other temperance killjoys. But more was to come.

It appears to us [the reader declaimed], that there can only be one possible reason why the increase of regular trade and of profit should not be carried still further, in

A barmaid of 1849 'pulling' pints. Bar pumps began to be installed in pubs in the first half of the nineteenth century. Before this, beer was drawn from a barrel behind the bar, or brought up from the cellar in jugs.

'Bobbing' or adulterating beer was common practice among some publicans, who could make two or three casks of inferior beer from one genuine cask delivered by the brewer. Added ingredients included salt and water; here, a block of salt is being thrown into the butt, while the assistant is mixing a compound called 'Black Jack', which sometimes contained treacle. The Illustrated London News described the practice as one that 'is principally carried on in "cheap neighbourhoods"; and may be considered as one of the evils of the Malt-Tax, as it would be scarcely worth while for the beer-seller to resort to adulteration if malt were free of duty.'

WHITBREAD PUBS TODAY
The Winchester Arms in
Taunton, Somerset, was built
as a private house in the
sixteenth century.

fact to the point at which the Brewery will be in full work, and that reason is that a very large further increase of trade might require a larger amount of capital. But a careful inspection of our accounts leads us to believe that we have now ample capital for a good increase of the trade. Even if this were not the case we think that the majority of the partners would be only too glad of the opportunity of adding to the amount they now have in the brewery.

The letter concluded with a 'very serious' objection to not expanding.

Viz that it produces an idea in the mind of every person in our employ that we do not want any more business and that there is no necessity for them to exert themselves. In fact it produces an indifference and a general slackness that is most detrimental to the interests of the business and that might be very difficult to remedy hereafter.

The vote that followed resulted in a victory for progress, but it was no coincidence that it was the first partners' meeting for John Martineau and Richard Worsley. It had taken their arrival to swing the balance of power. Without them, the action group would have had to have waited for the death of William Henry and his replacement by his son Samuel III the following year. Although even this might not have done the trick. Already in his mid-thirties, Sam III was firmly set on a political career that would see him the only member of the family to achieve office as Civil Lord of the Admiralty. His interest in the brewery was so slight that he would probably have abstained from any vote on its future management. Possibly the action party would have had to wait for the support of his younger brother William, who joined the partnership a few years later.

The real enthusiast for change was Francis Manning-Needham. Unlike his colleagues, he was a natural businessman and he was bursting with ideas for the brewery. For the record, it was his father who had initialled the critical letter, but it was young Francis who had inspired its contents.

The most radical of his new ideas was bottled beer.

Bottling was not a new concept. The attraction of a portable, hygienic, re-usable container in which beer would last indefinitely had been known for a very long time. The technology of glassmaking was equally ancient. The disadvantages had been economic. However, taxes on glass had been cut as long ago as 1834 and bottled beer was becoming more and more popular. The previous 30 years had seen another, much more revolutionary development, the railway. Railway mania had swept through the UK in the 1830s and 1840s and by 1866 every major city was connected to the network. For the first time there was a fast, cheap method of transporting bottled beer around the country.

Not that Francis Manning-Needham was looking that far ahead. But he had noticed that bottled beer labelled Bass and Worthington was beginning to arrive by rail from Burton-on-Trent and was proving very popular.

Now, with the new 'go-for-growth' policy, he could begin to put his plan for Whitbread to bottle its own beer into practice. Even so the partners decided to treat it as a separate venture and Francis had to rent a small

'The probable effect of Mr Somes's Sunday closing bill' from Punch, 1863.

A 'Spy' cartoon of Samuel III, published in Vanity Fair in 1895 : 'He has a paternal manner, and he brims over with virtuous sayings; which again have been flippantly called platitudes. . . . For he is a thoroughly good fellow as well as a good man of business.'

The first advertisements for Whitbread's bottled beer appeared in the 1870s. Advertisements at this time were typographical and not especially eye-catching, appearing on a page with others of the same style and aimed at trade customers.

A boot and flogger, used in the 1870s for corking bottles of beer. The boot, which held the bottle steady, was strapped to one thigh, while the flogger was used to bang the corks home.

warehouse about a quarter of a mile from the brewery, in Worship Street, in which to start bottling. Robert Baker was hired as its manager with a staff of two. One of these lieutenants was responsible for bottling Cooper and Extra Stout in Worship Street. The other, William Reeve, had to take his gang to Chiswell Street to bottle Whitbread's London Stout, Family Ale and Pale Ale, which were stacked in a cellar until they were in condition.

By the beginning of 1870 Baker was able to advertise in the *Licensed Victuallers' Guardian* that he had been appointed Whitbread's sole agent for their bottled beers and that he was ready to execute orders. Sales increased so fast that within three months the bottling plant had been moved to much larger premises in Gray's Inn Road, where William Reeve filled the first bottle on Easter Monday.

Bulk beer was brought over from Chiswell Street at the beginning of each week in butts which were set on stillions. The bottles were filled from lead-weighted siphons at the end of tubes from the butts. When the necks were inserted in the siphons, they automatically filled with beer. As many as 35,000 bottles, equal to 40 butts, were bottled in a day.

The bottles were then corked by hand, using what was known as a boot and flogger. One man could cork about 350 bottles a day, which meant a workforce of over a hundred by 1886, working nearly 12 hours a day. The attractions of automation were obvious, but it took ten years before the first effective corking-machine, a Worssam, capable of averaging 11,000 bottles a day, was installed. Another technical challenge was finding adequate corks. Only the best quality were used and by 1885 these were costing £3,000 a year. Screw stoppers began to be used in 1885, but some bottles were still being corked in 1920.

The bottles were labelled with Whitbread's trademark of a hind's head, printed and lettered in chocolate on an orange background. The company had suffered from forgery and the earliest labels read: 'Observe that the cork in this bottle is branded Whitbread and Co.' By the 1880s another instruction had been added: 'When empty, please destroy the label.' This was to stop the bottles being refilled with inferior ale. When screw stoppers were introduced, Whitbread covered them with paper capsules to thwart their removal before they reached the paying customer.

To begin with Whitbread only supplied its bottled beer to public houses, but it soon found the grocery trade was a better market. Demand grew fast, not only in and around London, where it could be supplied by dray, but also in the provinces. Bulk shipments could be made by canal to some regional markets, but most of the expanding industrial cities in the Midlands had to be supplied by rail. The beer for this trade was packed in cases of three dozen bottles, unpopular with customers because they were so heavy and with the railway staff because they were nailed shut. They were called coffins in Yorkshire, 'but to give Yorkshire people their due, they knew a good thing when they saw it and took to our beer from the very beginning'.

The Gray's Inn Road plant attracted predictably favourable comment from the trade press. 'Everything that ingenuity and capital can suggest or command,' wrote the *Aerated Waters Journal and Bottlers' Record* in 1885, 'has been provided to perfect the arrangements for the conduct of the business.' It was one way of putting it. In reality, of course, the new business was inventing itself as it went along, with Manning-Needham constantly asking for more money to finance expansion.

His pleas were bolstered by the way the success of bottled beer rubbed off on Chiswell Street, where production rose rapidly. By the middle of 1889, output was up to 336,000 barrels. To meet the new demand, however, meant further heavy investment. When Alfred Barnard, the author of *Barnard's Noted Breweries*, visited the brewery that summer, he immediately noted the new malt store,

> a substantial edifice which, with its lofty roof and turrets, towers high above the surrounding buildings. It was built on an improved principle, regardless of cost, from the designs of R. Mouland & Sons. The top storey, which is 140 feet from the ground, is reached by an enclosed zig-zag metal staircase springing from the ground floor. The solid workmanship of this building, which is constructed entirely of brick and iron, is most striking.

Barnard commented at length on the 'near perfect' arrangements for storing malt, including the 14 iron feeding-pipes, 'having the appearance of giant spider's legs, as big as a man's body'. Barnard found climbing the staircase rather fatiguing and was grateful to refresh himself with a draught of Whitbread's pale ale, which he declared compared most favourably with that manufactured in the 'Beer City', tasting well of the hop and looking both bright and sparkling. 'We also tasted the double stout,' the brewery writer reported, 'but found it too strong and heady for travellers.'

By the time his two-day visit ended, Barnard had noted every improvement to the brewery. They included a new tun-room, a second well, reaching down 327 feet, as by then so did the original one, both continuously pumped, two water reservoirs, each holding nearly 3,000 barrels on the roofs of two buildings, a new brewhouse, three refrigerators, one Morton and two Bennett's, capable of cooling 80 barrels an hour, the great fermenting-room, 165 feet long and 60 feet wide, with a single span roof, with next to it another as large in the course of erection, the 'workmen so numerous that the cellars looked like one vast beehive', the chainlift that

The hind's head as it appeared on Sam III's crest differs from the brewery's logo as shown on the bottle label. The head has been redrawn several times. This is one of the earliest bottles that still survives.

Illustrations of the Porter Tun-Room (left) and the North Yard (right) were published in 1889 in volume II of Barnard's Noted Breweries.

The Coach and Horses in the Strand, 1889. Many pubs were commissioned by publican owners rather than breweries. The resulting buildings were designed in a mixture of styles, often quite eccentric.

Louis Pasteur visited a number of breweries and studied yeasts through his microscope in a series of experiments to discover what caused fermentation, and why beers sometimes failed. Some of his research to determine the exact chemical processes that caused the fermentation of beer was carried out at Chiswell Street. Following Pasteur's work at Whitbread, the brewery established its own laboratory to examine yeasts and other substances. By 1920 this had become one of the major brewing laboratories in the world.

conveyed filled casks to the surface at the rate (if required) of 600 barrels an hour, and the railway dollies in the stores – 'it is wonderful how true they run, and how neatly they turn the corners; not one of them went off the line once during our visit and some of them made a journey of nearly a quarter of a mile.'

He added: 'We should be afraid to guess how many thousands of casks we saw stacked in tiers, almost to the ceiling, in these subterranean caves.' Barnard was also impressed by the new 70-horsepower Cowper steam engine that James Simpson & Co. had just installed in place of the old Boulton & Watt engine, which had served the brewery for almost exactly 100 years. And he waxed almost lyrical about Victor, one of the giant drayhorses, whom he met in the vast stables.

All this development, of course, was costing a great deal of money. More, much more, than the partners had envisaged 23 years earlier when they had been swayed by Francis Manning-Needham's arguments. It was nice that the expansion programme was going so well, particularly the new-fangled bottling business, but there was a limit to how much they wanted to invest, deep as some of their pockets were. The improvements to Chiswell Street alone had cost something like £50,000. And now young Manning-Needham and this new fellow Lubbock wanted to buy extra cellars in Britannia Street for all these bottles and were talking about expanding south of the river.

Edgar Lubbock had been a partner since 1875, when he had taken over the shareholding belonging to Lord Broughton, who had died in the late 1860s, shortly after William Henry Whitbread. He had become a firm ally of Francis Manning-Needham, particularly on the financial front where he was an expert. It was Lubbock to whom the partners turned for a solution to the problem.

Not that they really had to be told. The whole industry had been in a fervour of fund-raising for the last two years, ever since the Irish brewing firm of Guinness had shown the way at the end of 1886 by floating itself as a joint stock company with a capital of £4.5 million, a sum which, excitingly, had been subscribed many times over. Many smaller breweries immediately followed suit, with most finding eager buyers. 'There could not well be a surer sign that the public have no idea of abolishing the Brewing Trade, or a safer guarantee against future attacks, than the fact that large numbers of the general public are now partners in the general undertaking,' the *Brewing Trade Review* editorialized a year later, when the rush to sell shares was at its peak.

The bigger brewers held off a little longer, but it was not long before most of them, too, incorporated themselves under the 1862–86 Companies Acts. They realized they had no choice. The flood of new money was not only enabling their competitors to enlarge their capacity, it was also giving them the financial muscle to take over rival breweries and acquire their outlets. A serious outbreak of merger mania, in other words. Almost every brewery in the country raced to join.

Among the leading brewers to become limited companies in 1889 were Ansell, Courage, Friary, Truman Hanbury Buxton and Watney Combe Reid. Whitbread & Company Limited's Articles of Association were dated 24 July. The new company was given a capital of £1,250,000, equally divided into ordinary and preference shares, and a mortgage debenture stock of £750,000.

The ordinary shares were issued free of charge to Samuel Whitbread, Richard Godman, Frederick Godman, John Martineau, Richard Worsley, Edgar Lubbock, Henry William Whitbread and Charles Whitbread. They entitled them to all the existing assets of the brewery, valued at £1.7 million. The 4.5 per cent preference shares and the 4 per cent mortgage debentures were advertised for sale by Whitbread's new merchant bankers, Baring Brothers, at a premium of £2 per £100, payable by instalments of £10 on application, £27 on allotment and £65 on 12 September, to raise £1.3 million in new capital.

The issue was as successful as Barings had predicted.

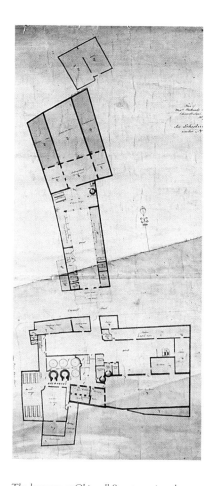

The brewery at Chiswell Street continued to expand on the north side of the street during the nineteenth century. When this map was drawn in 1867, the brewery still had not reached its maximum extent.

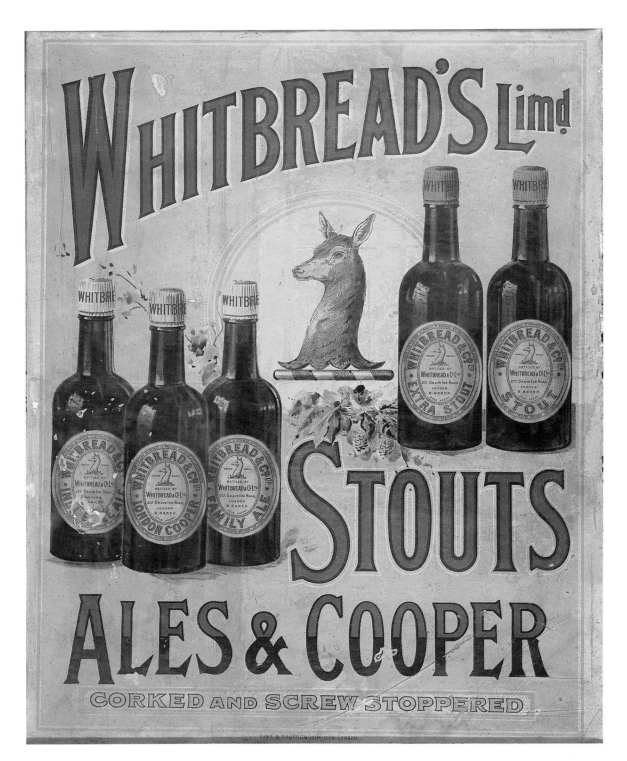

An early poster advertisement of the 1890s for
Whitbread beers.

CHAPTER SIX

SOME CORRESPONDENCE BETWEEN US

1889–1914

Samuel Whitbread III, it has to be said, took a good deal of persuading that turning the brewery into a limited company was a good idea. He still wasn't too happy about seeing his family name blazoned across all those bottles. But that paled into insignificance compared to the risk of it being dragged into the headlines due to some ill-judged business venture. Several safeguards had to be written into the Articles of Association before he would agree to the flotation. One was a clause which gave the family a 20-year option to stop the company using the name Whitbread if they felt it was being bought into disrepute. Another was the perpetual right of the founding shareholders to buy back ordinary shares issued to anyone apart from themselves and their direct descendants.

Even so there were loopholes, like the failure to specify precisely enough the right of young Whitbreads, Godmans, Martineaus, Lubbocks and Worsleys to become managing partners if they wanted to take an active part in the brewery's affairs. Young males, of course. Females weren't even allowed to own shares directly, let alone work in the family business.

A particular complainant was John Martineau. Right from the beginning he had felt that his shareholding in the new company was not worth as much as his original partnership. Five years later his resentment came to a head when he met resistance to his request that his son Maurice be made a managing director. On 22 February 1894 he wrote to Richard Worsley:

My dear Dick, With reference to the subject of our conversation the other evening, I have since accidentally come across some correspondence between us

in May 1889 which I think bears out the impression which was on my mind –
namely that as I was surrendering more in value than I was obtaining, the
compensation was to consist in the understanding that in all probability my son
would become a managing partner with more or less right to absorb [more capital].

Worsley replied on 8 March: 'Dear John, SW, Lubbock, HWW [Samuel
III's second son Henry William] and myself are all of the opinion that the
agreement that a part of your capital might be bequeathed to your son left
the question of his becoming a managing director open for future decision.
At the present time the number of managing directors is fully adequate to
the work to be done and it does not appear probable that any increase to the
managing direction will be required for a considerable period.'

Martineau wrote back in a fury. 'If it was in consequence of two new
managing directors having twice been admitted, why was I not told that in
giving my assent to their admission, which I did without any hesitation, I
was excluding my son?'

Worsley wrote to Harry Whitbread at the beginning of April: 'I am quite
content to let JM have the last word, if that is any satisfaction to him, in
this controversy.' But in the event it was not until March 1899 that the
argument was finally settled at an Extraordinary General Meeting which
amended the Article dealing with the rights of succession, including
cancelling the words: 'such son is to be precluded'. However, Maurice never
became a managing director.

There were other, more predictable, consequences to becoming a limited
company. One was an increase in paperwork. Right up to the end of the

A lively scene in a busy London pub of 1883.

A 1902 drawing of 'gentlemen from the Stock Exchange' refreshing themselves with the odd pint or two after a hard morning's dealing on the Floor.

partnerships Whitbread had managed to keep its clerical staff to a minimum. The counting-house, for example, only had four clerks in 1885 even though the total workforce was approaching 500. The working wage at Chiswell Street that year, incidentally, averaged 27s. a week. By the standards of the time the pay was good, as were the conditions of employment. There was a doctor on call and free funerals were introduced that year to employees who died in Whitbread's service. Sick pay of up to 2s. 6d. a day was allowed for occasional absence due to illness – except draymen. And everyone got free beer.

From 1889 onwards, however, the administrative staff inevitably increased, including a company secretary. If nothing else, somebody had to take the minutes at the new board meetings. The formalities, indeed, seemed to be endless, among them a company seal, which inevitably was a hind's head. But eventually the new board got down to real business with an offer at the end of 1890 for the Anchor Brewery in Lewisham.

The 60 years from 1830 to 1890 had seen a host of changes. The population explosion had continued unabated, with the total number of people living in England and Wales approaching 30 million. Real wages had doubled, a rise in wealth reflected in the huge expansion of London housing and a big jump in disposable income for a large percentage of the work-force.

Against this there had been the growing influence of the temperance movement and increasing attacks on the evils of drink, which were, it had to be confessed, still very prevalent. Although drunkenness had diminished among the ever more numerous middle classes, the absolute numbers of the poor were greater than ever. As was the consumption of alcohol, which had reached a peak in the mid-1880s of 34 million barrels of beer, wine and

A matchbox-holder from 1905 of a type used on tables or bars.

71

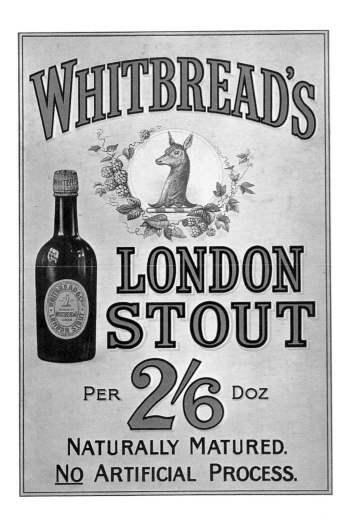

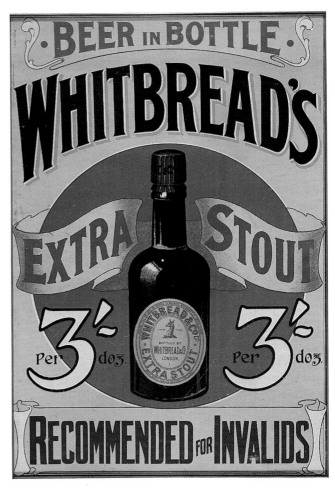

Two Whitbread Stout advertisements of c. 1910. They were displayed in off-licences, the underground and other public sites.

spirits. Although there had been a decline, the annual total was still 31 million barrels five years later.

Contributing to the fall was the Wine and Beerhouse Act of 1869, which had at last restricted unlicensed premises. A corollary, naturally, was a rise in the value of existing licences, which in turn encouraged brewers to invest more in the retail trade; in other words, the Act had given a new fillip to the tied-house system.

Altogether there were 103,000 public houses in England and Wales in 1890, equal to one for every 300 people in the population. But all the political and social signs were that this ratio would go down. With the rash of lucrative company flotations, the race to corner the pub market through mergers and acquisitions began in earnest.

Whitbread's directors were not particularly eager participants. The surprising success of their bottling business was taking them in a different direction. More by accident than design, Whitbread had become one of the pioneers of 'branded' beer, along with Worthington, Bass and one or two others, mostly based in Burton-on-Trent. This select group had discovered that there was a large market for high-quality bottled beer which sold at a premium and which transcended the barriers of the tied-house system. All

Whitbread pubs, for example, had been stocking Worthington since the mid-1870s, and its own bottled beers were fast achieving the same status outside London.

So one of the motives for buying the Anchor Brewery was to use its premises as a branch bottling-depot to serve the whole of Whitbread's London market south of the Thames. But the fact that the Anchor's tied trade of 24,000 barrels a year would largely transfer to Chiswell Street was another attraction. The asking price for the Lewisham brewery was £195,000. Edgar Lubbock beat the owners down to £185,000 and persuaded them to leave £60,000 of the purchase price on deposit with Whitbread.

Five years later Whitbread bought the Bell Brewery at Tottenham for £138,000, of which £76,000 was left on deposit. Once again the premises were converted into a bottling-plant and the business of supplying the Tottenham brewery's tied houses transferred to Chiswell Street. Next it bought a small brewery at Abridge in Essex. And in 1899 Whitbread moved westward with the takeover of Matthews & Cannings' brewery in Chelsea.

This deal was valued at £274,000 and included the hundred tied houses which took most of Matthews & Cannings' 60,000-barrel production. This time the brewery was kept open and Charles Crawshay, the manager and one of the owners, was made a managing director of Whitbread and employed to run it. Crawshay and his father were also issued with £57,000 worth of new ordinary shares in Whitbread, on condition that they had to be sold back to the company on the death of whichever of them survived longest, with 'no powers of absorbing'.

The expansion of bottling to Lewisham and Tottenham was only a small part of what was rapidly becoming a national network. Bottling had started in Birmingham and Leeds in 1892, followed the next year by Barnsley and

A Whitbread water-jug c. 1910, promoting Whitbread's bottled beers.

The Horseshoe and Wheatsheaf in Melior Street, London, was designed by W. T. Farthing in 1897. Now a freehold house called the Horseshoe Inn, the façade and interior remain unchanged, although the two bars have been knocked through into one.

A slate sign, advertising Whitbread Imperial Stout, which was fixed to the wall of a pub in the 1890s.

WHITBREAD PUBS TODAY
The Mayfly was originally a private cottage by the River Test in Hampshire. It was bought by Strong's brewery in 1907 and converted into a pub called the Seven Stars. It was renamed the Mayfly by Whitbread in 1976.

Liverpool. By 1900 Whitbread had bottling depots or stores in Sheffield, Cardiff, Manchester, Newcastle, Poole, Hull, Brighton, Bradford, Nottingham and Leicester, and sales of bottled beer were making a significant contribution to the company's profits, which, in view of the state of the rest of its business, was very fortunate.

The seeds of disaster for the brewing industry had been planted as long ago as 1892. That was when the House of Lords had rejected the appeal by Mrs Sharpe, the owner of a public house in a remote part of Westmorland, against her local magistrates for refusing to renew her licence. The right of JPs to cancel a publican's licence was finally enshrined in law. The judgement sent a chill wind through the trade, especially when it was followed by the Intoxicating Liquor Traffic (Local Control) Bill, the so-called 'Veto Bill', which gave house-owners the right to vote for total prohibition on the sale of drink in their local licensing area.

Local option, as it was called, was not a new idea. Sir Wilfred Lawson and other temperance supporters had been agitating for it for 20 years and a resolution in favour had been passed by the House of Commons in 1880. The judgement and the new Bill were potentially disastrous. They meant that at any moment the right of publicans to continue their business might be taken away, without any compensation. They undermined the whole basis on which the industry was built.

The danger took time to make itself felt. Whitbread's first ten years as a limited company showed continuous growth. By mid-1900 production was up to nearly 700,000 barrels and profits had climbed to £205,000.

But on the minus side of the balance sheet the cost of loans, outstanding interest, unpaid bills and rents owing had risen to more than £2.5 million. Whitbread had already issued the rest of its £1 million debenture stock. Now it was asking its shareholders to take up another £600,000 preference shares in order to finance expansion and replace short-term borrowings with permanent capital. The dividends payable on the new preference shares and the existing fixed interest stock were, the directors said, more than covered by net rents and mortgage interest from Whitbread's tied houses. What the prospectus did not spell out, because the directors did not suspect it, was just how vulnerable this income was about to become.

By 1900 an estimated 95 per cent of all public houses had become tied in one way or another, either through breweries owning their leaseholds or through loans to publicans to pay for improvements or stock. Not to mention outstanding bills and discounts on the brewery's wholesale price for draught beer, still selling for only 4*d.* a quart retail in spite of a recent increase in duty. Luckily this had been offset by a fall in the price of hops and in any case the Chancellor of the Exchequer had promised that it was a temporary rise in tax to meet the unexpected cost of the little police action in the Transvaal against the Boers. Thanks to the growth of its bottled beer trade, Whitbread was less dependent on its tied trade than many of its competitors, but even so something like 50 per cent of its beer production went to pubs with which it had a financial connection.

The first hard evidence that the situation was changing for the worse came early in the new century when magistrates throughout the country

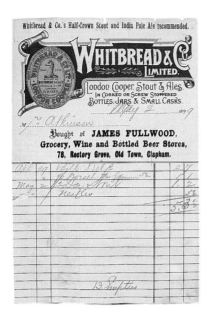

An order for Whitbread's bottled beer dated 2 May 1899.

A match-striker and holder, made about 1905 and used on pub bars.

began to use the power to refuse licences that the judgement against Mrs Sharpe had given them. In more reflective moments even the brewers had to admit that they were sometimes justified. Too many pubs were unsavoury places, little better than drinking dens. Improvement was clearly desirable.

But the arbitrary refusal of licences was equally obviously unjust. The Brewers' Society rallied its forces and persuaded the Home Secretary to introduce a Bill entitling publicans who lost their licences to compensation unless it was for misconduct. The Prime Minister, Arthur Balfour, summed up the arguments for the Bill in the House:

You will never get rid of the public house from this country and, I frankly admit it, I do not think you ought to get rid of it. What then should you aim at? Surely at this ideal, that the public house should be kept respectably, should be kept by respectable persons and should be kept in such a manner as will make those who frequent it obey the law and conform to the dictates of morality; a difficult ideal to attain, but one which never seems to occur to a certain class of temperance reformer. Their one desire seems to be to render the tenure of the publican insecure. How can you expect the trade which you deliberately intend to make insecure to be filled by men of the character I have just endeavoured to describe?

The Act, which was passed in 1904, pleased no one, from the Liberal opposition, which had embraced the temperance cause as its own, calling it the Brewers' Endowment Bill, to the publicans who resented having to finance local compensation, dubbing it the 'Mutual Burial Fund'. But if nothing else it made some brewers think about improving their pubs.

At Whitbread, the question was taken seriously. Part of the trouble, it was decided, was the absence of decent food in pubs. The idea won the support of the managing directors, who now included Harry Whitbread and Edgar Lubbock's nephew Cecil. Whitbread signed a contract with the Central Catering Company of 100 Theobald's Road to supply food to its public houses. By October 1905, about 400 were being supplied daily.

Whitbread was so enthusiastic about the scheme that it decided to take over the Central Catering Company and extend its services to all the brewery's tied houses. A letter from Percival Grundy, Whitbread's company secretary, told publicans that the new subsidiary would 'shortly be in a position to supply all articles of food and appliances for catering on modern methods'. And it added: 'You are particularly requested to exercise care in ordering, as on and after the 6th November the Central Catering Company will discontinue taking back returns.'

The last comment was a sign that the venture was already in trouble. It only took a year to reveal how badly. A private memorandum to the shareholders in November 1906 revealed that the Central Catering Company was running at an annual loss of nearly £10,000 before depreciation. It went on: 'When the Central Catering Company was started the managing directors looked upon it as an excellent step from the licensing point of view and they *now* attach great importance to the food trade being done and being encouraged in all the houses where it is possible to do so. But for the following reasons they are now unanimous in the opinion that the Central Catering Company had better be sold or wound up as soon as possible.'

The reasons ran to ten, all of them negative. They included the discovery that a good deal more food trade was being done in Whitbread's pubs than its managing directors had any idea of; that publicans preferred to do their own catering; that it was impossible to supply food from outside to all the pubs at the exact moment each of them wanted it, which meant high returns; and that the economics of outside supply were terrible. 'The loss on the Central Catering Company could only be justified if we can show it is to the assistance of the publican, which we had expected and which it is not, and also if we could then get a large addition of trade of a paying kind, which nearly two years' experience has shown us to be impossible.'

It was a salutary lesson in the importance of market research.

The decision to close the ill-fated catering operation was signed by Frank Whitbread, Harry's younger brother, who had been a director for 14 years. Aged 40, he was in the middle of a two-year stint as chairman of the Brewers' Society and also chaired the National Trade Defence Association, which had been formed in 1888 to protect the interests of brewers and publicans, beginning with support for Mrs Sharpe's appeal. A barrister, he had become one of the principal spokesmen for the industry in its increasingly desperate fight against repressive controls of licences.

For the Liberals had won the last election and a new attack was developing. It appeared the next year in the form of the 1907 Licensing Bill, which proposed to limit the right of renewal of licences to 14 years. If it passed into law, it would amount to an act of confiscation, as public houses were valued on the assumption that their licences were, subject to good conduct, effectively permanent.

To the delight of the trade, the Bill sparked the most startling opposition from the general public. There was an outcry in the press, MPs were deluged with letters and protest meetings all over the country. There were several

Frank Whitbread, painted in 1927. A lawyer by training, he was a tireless spokesman for the brewing industry for many years.

The Old Dover Castle (below left) and the Rising Sun (below right) were both designed by Treadwell & Maxwell and built in London in the 1890s. Late Victorian pub interiors were spectacular and spacious places, with elaborate cut glass and extravagant decor, which provided an escape from the drabness of everyday life. These two pubs were particularly sophisticated. In the Old Dover Castle, patrons of the saloon bar could drink mulled claret or soup at the bar, before slipping into the adjoining restaurant for something more substantial.

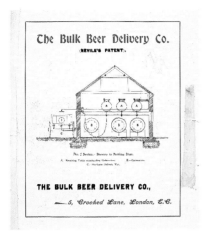

A poster illustrating Sydney Nevile's prototype horse-drawn beer-tanker, c. 1900. This was the first time that beer was carried in tanks rather than casks – although an apparently obvious idea, it took the arrival of commercial motor vehicles and other developments in beer distribution before bulk transport became widely used.

by-elections during the Bill's progress through the Commons, all of which the Government lost by crushing margins. The storm of protest culminated in a monster rally in Hyde Park on 27 September 1908, attended by half a million people, many of them travelling into London on special trains. In the face of such massive opposition, the Bill could only fail.

One of the minor players in the fight was a young head brewer called Sydney Nevile, who led a contingent of 250 employees from his Putney brewery to the rally and co-authored a pamphlet on the evils of local option which sold several thousand copies. Nevile, an energetic advocate of improving public houses, advanced the novel concept that there was no conflict between the permanent commercial interest of the brewing trade and the best interests of the public. Never afraid to air his views, Nevile bluntly stated that brewers could make more money out of England sober than England drunk and that reform was only enlightened self-interest.

His views attracted the attention of Frank Whitbread and Cecil Lubbock, both of whom already knew him as keenly interested in quality control and technical advances in beermaking. One of young Sydney's more novel ideas had been a prototype horse-drawn beer-tanker holding 360 gallons. Now he was talking intelligently if provocatively about raising standards in public houses.

He was not the only one. Some brewers had even begun to take action. Charringtons, for example, had persuaded the justices in one south-east London borough to let them double the size of one of their pubs, with the new half selling soft drinks and refreshments only. The experiment proved before its time, perhaps in part because the chairs were very upright – the objection to more comfortable seating was that it would be difficult to judge the sobriety of lounging customers. Whitbread's own ill-fated foray into catering had been another attempt to make pubs more attractive.

Something had to be done, because the situation had been deteriorating ever since 1901, when the economic depression had begun to take hold.

A bird's-eye view of the Chiswell Street brewery about 1900, when it was at its fullest extent. On the south side (right) was the brewery, the main offices and some stables. The north side (far right) contained the depot, with the cooperage and distribution areas.

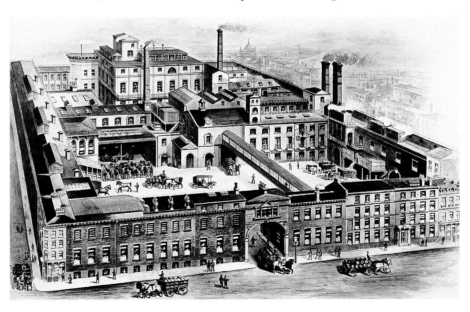

The mill room in Chiswell Street at the turn of the century, where the barley was milled.

Whitbread's profits had peaked at £246,000, but had fallen for the next five years, in spite of record beer output. The problem was bad debts.

Up to 1905, the company reckoned it had done well and could boast that although its capital had increased greatly, it was selling the same number of barrels per £1,000 capital as it had been in 1890. 'The whole brewery premises and plant are now in a thoroughly efficient state and the freehold area is over five acres,' the directors reported. But that didn't stop them having to cut the ordinary dividend due to the high price of hops and heavy write-offs, including £161,000 for bad debts and depreciating pub values.

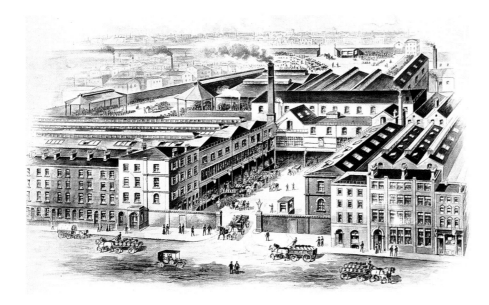

The opening of the Brussels depot with, from left to right, Messrs Parsons, Richardson, Sharpe and Fox. Right: *The Brussels depot in full working order, after it had opened.*

Three years later sales fell for the first time for 20 years due to the 'great and general depression of trade in London'. With profits down to £164,000 the directors waived their preference dividends and converted their £474,000 holdings of preference shares into ordinary shares, cancelling £300,000 of the latter into the bargain.

This was in response to a boardroom study the previous year which had concluded that Whitbread needed to write off at least £150,000 a year for the foreseeable future. The only question was whether profits would be high

A motor dray in Ypres beside the ruins of the cathedral, photographed in 1919, just after the First World War.

enough to cover this rate of depreciation and pay dividends. The answer was probably, provided some unforeseen calamity did not occur.

Within a year it had, in the form of a crushing increase in licence duties in the 1908 Budget, the Government's revenge on the beer trade for defeating the Licensing Bill. From a maximum of £60 a year, the licence duty went up to several hundreds for big houses. The impact on the London trade was particularly savage and the major brewers were forced to push up the price of beer from 4*d.* to 5*d.* a quart for the first time for almost a hundred years. Another political row ended with the Lords throwing the Budget out.

Although this brought the price of beer down again, it did nothing to ease the pressure publicans and brewers were under. By 1911 Whitbread had been forced to write more than £1 million off its loans and the dividend on the ordinary shares was only half a per cent. By then the licensing laws had finally been consolidated. But so, too, had licence duties, with the result that Whitbread was impelled to write £300,000 off the value it placed on its public houses. By the middle of 1914, the company's total assets were a million pounds below their 1905 peak.

About the only good news was the continued success of the bottled-beer business. Since 1900 Whitbread bottling-depots had been established throughout the UK and in 1904 the company had opened its first overseas depot, in Brussels. Two years after that it had expanded to Antwerp, by which time Whitbread's UK bottling empire had branches in Glasgow, Southend and the Isle of Wight. In 1910 bottling began in Dundee and Liège. Paris opened in 1912 and Ghent in 1913. By then more than half the brewery's output of nearly one million barrels a year was being bottled and Whitbread & Co. had become the greatest beer-bottler in the land.

THE HOP GARDENS OF KENT
BY MOTOR-BUS

GENERAL

The hop-gardens of Kent were a popular
destination for a day trip from London, as well
as supplying the capital's breweries with the
bulk of their hops.

CHAPTER SEVEN

NO GUARANTEE

1914–1929

The Great War changed the lives of everyone. At Whitbread, as in every company in Great Britain, the initial impact was the abrupt departure of most of its unmarried young men into the Armed Forces. Like many boards, Whitbread's directors responded to their patriotism by continuing to pay their salaries in full for a month, followed by three months at half pay, and promising to keep their jobs open. Three months later it extended the half-salary period to six months and by July the next year it was offering the same inducement to married men.

Clerks in the bottling-plants were not treated so generously. All they were offered was two months' salary and the promise of their jobs back if possible, 'but under existing circumstances no guarantee of this can be given'.

The existing circumstances were the realization that the war was not going to be over for a long time and the increasing difficulties of the industry. Lloyd George, the Prime Minister of the Coalition Government, had already increased the duty on beer from 7s. 9d. to 23s. a barrel. He had taken the advice of Cecil Lubbock, who had told him that the new duty would probably reduce sales by 20 per cent, which was about the amount that the brewers expected their output to fall due to restrictions on supplies. The Prime Minister accepted Lubbock's advice. Beer rose from 2d. to 3d. a pint and the brewers nervously anticipated a sharp fall in demand. The war effort, however, created full employment and rising wages and the industry's fears were not fulfilled.

Production was, however, curtailed to 18 million barrels at the beginning of 1917 and halved again, to less than a third of pre-war output, in March. Consumption was already being limited by the Defence of the Realm (Amendment) No. 3 Act, which had called into being the Central Control Board (Liquor Traffic) with far-reaching powers. Among its actions was the

Nos 5 and 6 platoons (Whitbread & Co), part of 2/6th Battalion, County of London in 1917. More than a thousand Whitbread employees served in the First World War, of whom 95 were killed in action or died from their wounds.

The great storage vats were dismantled in 1918 and the area became part of the cooperage.

limitation of opening hours from nineteen and a half hours a day in London to five and a half. Another development was a fall in the alcohol content of strong ale from around 5 per cent to nearer 3 per cent. This was due more to the desire to make limited supplies of malt go further than any government controls, but the effect was the same. The Board also encouraged meals in pubs as an antidote to drunkenness among munition workers.

There were other, more alarming proposals, such as the nationalization of brewing and public houses. The threat sprang out of the need to preserve crops of barley for bread and animal feed. As Master of the Brewers' Company and chairman of the London Brewers' Council, Lubbock led the industry's fight against it. At Lloyd George's suggestion, a small committee was set up to discuss nationalization with Lord Milner, who would be in charge of implementing it. Representing the metropolitan brewers was Sydney Nevile. The idea faded, to be replaced by a demand for beer production to be concentrated in a few breweries to save fuel. Nevile, on behalf this time of the Institute of Brewing, pressed the opinion that fuel savings could be achieved just as efficiently by the industry as it was. The Government rewarded him by demanding a reduction of 25 per cent. The target was met, although not without pain.

Resilient demand in spite of high prices meant that Whitbread's profits during the war rose almost embarrassingly to nearly £200,000 in 1917. Excess profits tax kept them at about this level from then on, but that still left the board with enough to pay hardship bonuses to its staff, at a rate of 10 per cent on salaries below £300 a year and 7.5 per cent between £300 and £900. For 1917 the bonuses totalled just under £20,000, with a tenth of that going to 'female clerks, women and boys'.

The worst suffering was in flesh and blood. The demand for fresh troops was endless. By the middle of 1916 Whitbread was offering six months' full salary and half salary after that to all married men of military age who joined up, whether they worked in the brewery or the bottling-stores. By January 1917 the full-salary period was up to nine months.

By the end of the war 1,071 of Whitbread's employees had enlisted. Out of their number, 95 had been killed in action or died from wounds. They included Captain Frederick Godman of the Royal Sussex Regiment, who had been taken prisoner at the Battle of Loos in September 1915 and had died in captivity three years later.

The aftermath of the war found Whitbread, like the country at large, in a weakened state. It was particularly short of expert management. Like his uncle Edgar, Cecil Lubbock was as much a financier as a brewer, with directorships at the Bank of England and Northern Assurance, as well as membership of the City of London Income Tax Commissioners and the Council of Foreign Bond Holders. Percy Grundy, promoted from company secretary, was a 'loyal clerk'. And Harry Whitbread, although he had been a managing director for more than 20 years and was devoted to the family business, was not a leader. The solution, Lubbock told the board, was an outside appointment. And he recommended Sydney Nevile.

Nevile was keen to accept. For one thing, his old job was in jeopardy. Chester Brandon, the heir to the Putney brewery in which Nevile was head brewer, had been killed in the Middle East and his father wanted to sell up. Nevile had, in fact, tried to interest Whitbread in buying, but Lubbock had jibbed at the price. He had, as Nevile recorded later, 'experienced difficulties in those lean years around 1900 which had made him somewhat pessimistic and unduly cautious'.

Nevile was the very opposite. Endlessly energetic and irrepressibly enthusiastic, he had a catholic knowledge of the brewing industry and a plethora of ideas about improving it which he was bursting to put into effect, from better beer to better pubs. The war had seen him become a personal adviser to Lloyd George as well as a spokesman for the industry. Eight years younger than Frank Whitbread, at 45 Nevile was at the height of his powers, as well as one of the best-known brewers in the industry. At a salary of £2,500, plus an annual bonus of £1,500 dependent on profits, he was a bargain.

He was also something of a shock, especially to Percy Grundy, who was a dyed-in-the-wool traditionalist, deeply hurt by any implication that the historic methods and usages of Whitbread's were less than perfect. The ebullient Nevile teased the elderly Grundy cruelly.

The new managing director's first task was to help complete the purchase of a hop farm. Beltring, near Paddock Wood in Kent, had belonged to a near-genius hop-grower called Albert White who had developed a prize-winning variety called 'White's Golding'. For many years Whitbread had bought the bulk of his crop. Continuity of flavour was thought essential to beer-making and on White's death Whitbread hurried to make an offer for the 440-acre farm, before it could fall into the hands of a competitor.

Nevile and Lubbock were shown round Beltring by White's adopted son Waghorn. Afterwards they retired to consider the price. Sydney suggested a lower offer. Cecil looked offended. It was not the Whitbread way to haggle, he explained. Nevile persuaded him to bend his principles to the extent of making a firm offer £10,000 below the asking price. It only took Waghorn one telephone call before he accepted. Sydney wondered to himself afterwards how much lower a little real haggling might have pushed the price finally agreed.

Like other hop-gardens Beltring suffered ups and downs, but over the years it proved a satisfactory investment, as well as a most picturesque addition to the brewery. Four thousand Eastenders spent their annual

Enamelled iron advertisements of this type were extensively used, especially at railway stations, from around 1920.

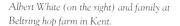

Albert White (on the right) and family at Beltring hop farm in Kent.

The oast houses and hop-pickers at the Beltring hop farm at the turn of the century.

Hop-pickers in the hop-gardens, from an album of photographs taken by a hop-picker's family.

WHITBREAD PUBS TODAY
The Buddle Inn on the Isle of Wight was granted its first licence in 1850 and bought in 1874 by Mew, Langton, Isle of Wight brewers who were acquired by Strong's of Romsey in 1965. Strong's were taken over by Whitbread in 1969.

holidays picking hops at Beltring and many thousands of sightseers visited the farm with its rows of 'bines' and its tip-tilted kilns.

Another early deal was the purchase of just under 80 per cent of the ordinary shares of a wines and spirits merchant called Stowell & Sons for £20,000. Following its acquisition, the company made a profit of £5,000 in 1921 and, more to the point, raised its purchases of Whitbread beer from £5,000 the year before to £11,000.

Nevile reported these results to the board on 8 May 1922. He continued with some slightly less satisfactory news about the pet project that he had persuaded his new employer to finance, the Improved Public House Company, founded in October 1920 and reporting for the first time.

Sydney Nevile had been expanding his thesis on the commercial as well as social benefits of lifting standards in public houses ever since his address to the Brewers' Society 13 years earlier. His opinions had been strengthened by what was commonly known as the Carlisle Scheme. Although nationalization of public houses had been abandoned during the war, the Central Control Board had used its powers to take over the licensed trade in three districts of Britain, one of which was Carlisle on the Anglo-Scottish border. The Board, of which Nevile was a member, had acquired Carlisle's five breweries and all their public houses. It closed four of the breweries and many of the pubs. But it greatly improved the ones it kept. Better ventilation and lighting, more seating, meals, music and other recreations; even separate rooms for women, a much-criticized innovation. The Board's success in Carlisle owed much to the limits state control put on drinking by munition workers from Glasgow, shorter hours, weaker beer and spirits and higher prices. But it was striking.

Nevile was in any case firmly convinced that improvement was good business and he persuaded Whitbread to let him make his point in practice.

MR HUNN
HON SECRETARY.

Above and opposite: Caricatures from the
House of Whitbread, *the company magazine
started by Nevile, which was filled with news
items and features covering company events,
character sketches, corporate announcements,
company gossip, and launches of new products
and lines.*

The Welcome Inn at Eltham in Kent was the
first of Whitbread's new Improved Public
Houses to be built in the early 1920s. Still
owned by Whitbread, it is now a Beefeater
Restaurant.

A 1920s motor lorry kept at Whitbread's
Marlow depot.

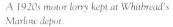

It proved an expensive experiment. One problem was that magistrates
stubbornly refused to allow existing pubs to be enlarged, seeing the
additions only as extra drinking space. So Nevile was forced to build new
pubs. The first was the Welcome Inn at Eltham. It included a large concert
hall, a separate flat for the manager and his wife, and individual
accommodation for all the staff. Nevile persuaded Sir Kingsley Wood, the
local MP, to open Whitbread's first Improved Public House and held a
reception with 300 guests at which he made an impassioned speech about
the value of a good public house to its community.

In the privacy of Whitbread's boardroom, though, Nevile had to confess
that the new company had been faced with the expenses and difficulties
associated with a new concern and some loss was natural. So far as
purchases from Whitbread were concerned, those by Improved Public
Houses were 6 per cent better by volume and 9 per cent better in cash terms
than the average for company houses. Nevile did not, however, regard the
situation as satisfactory and, although he felt that the enterprise should be
continued, he promised to strive for a substantial commercial return.

Sydney had established himself well enough at Whitbread to have his
judgement accepted. He had already made his mark in the brewery,
especially on transport. Whitbread still stabled nearly 300 horses at
Chiswell Street under the care of John Lomax, who had been the transport
manager since 1896.

It was quite a sight [Nevile recorded] in the evening to watch the unharnessing of
the horses and see them going each to its own stall in the brewery stables. The

WHIST WENT WEST

J DIVER PUTTING THE
HALF PENNIES TO BED

Whitbread hired steam wagons to transport heavy consignments of beer from the brewery to the bottling depots.

stalls were on three floors, with access by ramps which naturally had to be fairly steep. Each horse knew its own stall, but occasionally a newcomer might find its way into one belonging to another horse – this was apt to occur if the newcomer to the team arrived home early – and then there would be pandemonium; for when the rightful occupant appeared and found his stall had been filched from him, he would at once take the nearest one which captured his fancy and the result was something like a game of musical chairs, with horses charging here there and everywhere in search of empty stalls.

It had been obvious for some time that motor transport had to take the place of the horses to save costs and space at the brewery. So far, however, the only move Whitbread had made in the direction of mechanization was the hire of steam wagons to deliver especially heavy consignments of beer to bottling-depots.

Nevile's advice was awaited. One problem was the large number of old draymen, who might have found the speed of petrol vehicles too great after the leisurely pace of their horses. Nevile's compromise was a fleet of electric vehicles made by Ransomes Sims & Jefferies of Ipswich. With a load of

Below left: Electric transport was used at Chiswell Street from 1920 to 1948. These vehicles had a top speed of 10 miles per hour and were ideal for short-range deliveries.

Below: A lorry at the Bristol depot decorated for the Calne carnival in 1927.

Cecil Lubbock (left) and Harry Whitbread in the 1930s.

Local off-licences delivered beer by tricycle – but not usually as elaborately decorated as this one from Mandeville Stores in Enfield Wash.

2.5 tons and a top speed of 10 miles an hour, the new wagons worked well enough as substitutes for horse-drawn drays around Chiswell Street, although it wasn't long before Whitbread was using petrol and diesel engines.

Another Nevile development was tankers for deliveries of bulk beer to the bottling-stores, although they were a big advance on his experiment in Putney. And he had just scored a personal triumph following the 1921 coal strike, which had left Whitbread short of fuel.

Fatalistically, Cecil Lubbock had decided that as all brewers must be in the same boat, the only answer was to brew less and ration beer supplies to pubs. To his horror, Sydney learned that most of Whitbread's bigger competitors were planning full production. He persuaded his colleagues to give him *carte blanche* to avert the risk of being caught short. He rang up Sir John Thorneycroft, a connection by marriage and the head of the engineering firm, and asked if he knew of a war-surplus oil-burning plant, perhaps from a disused destroyer. Thorneycroft told him that the Slipway Company had suitable burners in Newcastle, a pressure pump could be bought in Glasgow and a firm of junk dealers in the East End had boilers which could be used as an oil reservoir. Sydney arranged special deliveries from the North and drove to Bermondsey, where the dealer, looking anywhere but in his eye, said he would 'enter into any arrangement that would lead to business'. Nevile agreed his price and within a week Chiswell Street was operating on oil.

Nevile had also begun to revitalize Whitbread's staff. The senior employees – Henry Field the head brewer, Walter Sharpe who had succeeded Robert Baker as head of the bottling division and was largely responsible for its development into a national network, latterly with the help of his nephew Granville Sharpe and Percy Grundy's brother Arthur, and William

Esse, the head 'abroad-cooper' and a keen supporter of public-house improvement – were all highly experienced and competent men. But there was no policy of recruiting educated young men to train to take their places. Cecil Lubbock, an old Etonian, as were the three Whitbreads on the board, was a firm believer in the value of a classical education as the best foundation for success in life. Nevile, whose elder brothers had also been to Eton – like the original Samuel Whitbread, Sydney's apprenticeship at 16 had been caused by the death of his father – deferred. The results, he confessed later, were not uniformly successful. When one young man whom Lubbock had promised a job at the brewery arrived fresh from Cambridge, Nevile told him that the best he was prepared to offer was a year's unpaid experience which might help him get a paid job somewhere else. 'I'm sorry to say, young man,' Sydney pronounced magisterially, 'that we already employ two graduates from your university. They seem to spend most of their time in night clubs and are too tired to get up for mashing in the morning.'

None of these developments did much to alter the fundamental circumstances affecting Whitbread's business. The end of the war had left beer much weaker and more expensive – 7d. a pint – than it had been five years earlier. The post-war economic boom had been reflected in beer sales, but prices had stayed high, due in large part to further huge increases in duty, from 23s. a barrel to 70s. in 1920 and 100s. in 1922. It fell back to 80s. in 1924, largely due to Nevile's intercession with the Chancellor, but consumption stayed at around 24 million barrels a year, about 20 per cent below pre-war levels.

Another constraint on the industry was the continuation of restrictions on opening hours. The 1921 Licensing Act set the hours during which intoxicating liquor could be sold during the week in London at nine hours a day, and eight elsewhere, with a limit of five hours on Sundays, Christmas Day and Good Friday, except for Wales and Monmouthshire, where there was no Sunday opening. Even more of a problem was the continued erosion of licences. Whitbread was not the only brewer to find many magistrates

Whitbread 'zeppelin' advertisement of the early 1920s.

An off-licence in Southsea in 1925, with a large display of Whitbread's bottled beers in the left-hand window. Off-licences were encouraged to mount imaginative window displays featuring Whitbread's products by the possibility that a picture of their shopfront might be featured in the House of Whitbread.

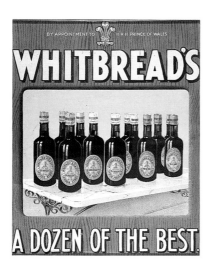

A Whitbread advertisement from the 1920s.

An Edwardian jardinière, now extremely rare, advertising Whitbread's bottled beer.

only prepared to allow improvements at one pub in exchange for the surrender of the licence for another. The effect was inevitable. Once again brewers found themselves pushed into competition for retail outlets and the merger game was back in fashion.

Whitbread's first move was reactive rather than aggressive. The owner of the Forest Hill Brewery in south London, Edward Venner, asked Nevile if Whitbread would like to buy it as he was about to become the chairman of another brewery. By the end of May 1923 three-quarters of Forest Hill's shareholders had accepted Whitbread's offer.

Characteristically, Sydney was attracted to the new brewery for technical reasons. Although Whitbread's bottled beers had an excellent reputation, the fact that they 'matured in bottle' meant that sediment was inevitable. Forest Hill, however, had built up a considerable trade in the increasingly popular 'bright' beer, which was matured and filtered before bottling.

The takeover resulted in the closure of the south London brewery, which involved making Forest Ale, as the beer was labelled, elsewhere. Nevile and Carl Wootton, the bottling expert he had hired to advise the technically untutored Walter Sharpe and his staff, paid an inquisitive visit to the two great Copenhagen breweries, Tuborg and Carlsberg. Then the two of them designed a small bright-beer plant which they erected in the redundant Gray's Inn Road bottling-depot. After some teething pains, they found that Whitbread's beer, 'being brewed from exceptionally good material', responded well to the new treatment. With great trepidation, the new method was applied to the Whitbread brand, although to avoid upsetting traditional drinkers it was kept in store for a month before distribution. There was only one complaint, and that was from a drinker who was convinced the sediment had had medicinal value.

The immediate value of the new acquisition, however, was the extra outlets it brought. Their appetite whetted, the managing directors of Whitbread were swift to seek out new prey. The prospect of buying a largish London brewery for £400,000 came to nothing. So did an attempt to buy the Rock Brewery in Brighton a couple of years later, although negotiations dragged on tantalizingly. But a bid of £270,000 for the Kent brewery of Frederick Leney & Sons, with 130 pubs, most of them freehold, was successful. Nevile stated that the deal was cheaper than Rock would have been, as the price worked out at £11. 14s. per barrel as compared with £15.

But the overall business situation did not look so good. Between 1920 and 1926 Whitbread's draught trade had fallen by 40 per cent and sales of bottled beer had dropped by 20 per cent. The average fall overall was 34 per cent, twice the decline experienced by the trade as a whole. 'This shrinkage', Cecil Lubbock told the board, 'means a loss of income amounting to £180,000 a year, or capitalized not less than £1,500,000. I think the seriousness of these figures will convince everyone that the time has come for drastic action. The only remedy I can think of which will have a far-reaching effect is an amalgamation, a conclusion which most of the big brewers seem to have already arrived at.'

Sydney Nevile explained that there had been a great migration of people from the inner city, where Whitbread's houses were situated, to the outer suburbs of London. A large part of its free bottled-beer trade had disappeared because almost every brewer now sold his own brand. And public demand for draught beer was falling steadily, helped in the recent past by a run of poor quality. The only hope was to strengthen Whitbread's sales methods and improve the management of its pubs. And he was strongly of the opinion that additional outlets must be acquired.

The company had the resources to embark on further acquisitions, although he recommended employing an adviser with 'intimate and continuous knowledge of the financial methods and arrangements in other brewery companies'. Challengingly he concluded: 'If the managing directors are to be successful they must not only have a policy but that policy must receive the united confidence and support of the whole board.' The relevance of this Parthian shot was revealed at the next board meeting, when Sydney explained that a merger involving two breweries with a combined output of 250,000 barrels, 'which he would call XY', had been torpedoed by Temple Godman, one of the largest shareholders, who would not contemplate any proposals which involved the issue of debentures as well as cash.

A behind-the-scenes power struggle ended with the managing directors authorized to negotiate a marriage with the Cannon Brewery. But this courtship, too, came to nothing.

So did a bid for a Maidstone brewery. But in 1929 Whitbread was offered some public houses in the Weald of Kent owned by Jude Hanbury, which had recently moved its brewery to Canterbury in anticipation of the Channel Tunnel bringing industrial expansion to East Kent. The proceeds of the sale would help Jude Hanbury pay for the Hythe brewery of Mackeson. Nevile thought the price being asked for the mid-Kent pubs was much too high. Instead he proposed a merger of Jude Hanbury and Mackeson with Leney & Sons, with Whitbread providing the finance and keeping a majority share in the combine and Jude Hanbury's management to run it. Another spin-off, naturally, was that the pubs throughout the new group should stock Whitbread bottled beer as well as their own brands. The plan went through, but had hardly taken effect before the worst financial blizzard the world had ever experienced broke across the British economy and forced the minority shareholders to sell out to Whitbread.

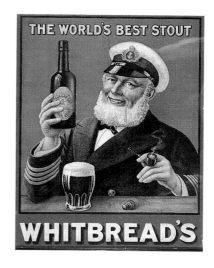

An advertisement from the 1920s, showing the healthy benefits of drinking stout.

Many early Whitbread bottles were embossed with the name and the hind's head, like the bottle on the left. This practice finally ceased in the 1940s. Labels were used throughout to indicate the brand.

*Sydney Nevile, painted by Patrick Phillips. The
painting was commissioned by the Brewers'
Company, of which Nevile was Master in 1929.*

CHAPTER EIGHT

WHEN YOU'RE WITH WHITBREADS YOU'RE FREE

1929–1945

The Great Depression is one of the anomalies of British history. In the short term it was a disaster which halved steel output and cotton exports, brought shipbuilding to a standstill, increased unemployment to three million and forced Britain off the Gold Standard.

But a longer view from 1913 to 1939 shows most people in the country becoming steadily better off. By the start of the Second World War the average standard of living had risen by something like a third.

What this overall figure conceals is that some sectors of the economy, largely the old smokestack industries, were beginning their long decline while other areas, like chemicals, plastics, electrical goods and motor transport, were bursting into luxuriant bloom. Coupled with a boom in cheap housing and the mass production of small cars, the new industries had laid the foundations of middle-class affluence for many.

Unluckily for Whitbread and its rivals, beer was one of the losers. Whitbread's production, which had fallen to 400,000 barrels in 1918, was only 100,000 barrels higher 11 years later. This was no better or worse than the industry in general. The brewers were caught between the tendency of the better-off to spend their disposable income on other things than beer and the sheer inability of unemployed working men to afford even the cheapest pint.

Whitbread was not as vulnerable as many regional brewers, but it had not been a major winner in the recent bout of acquisitions, thanks to the reluctance of major shareholders to increase borrowings. Sales of bottled

Full or empty, Whitbread bottles had many uses.

beer were also falling, especially in the North. And the company's position was further weakened by the fact that too many of its tied houses were in the poorer parts of London. Any independent appraisal of Whitbread's prospects at the beginning of the 1930s could only have been extremely cautious.

Except for the presence of Sydney Nevile. In both senses of the word. By then in his mid-fifties, Nevile was a national figure; Master of the Brewers' Company, on the Council of the Federation of British Industries, independent adviser to the Royal Commission on Licensing, past President of the Institute of Brewing, consultant to government departments – the list went on and on. Few people in the industry could claim to be better qualified than Nevile in the art or, as he had increasingly made it, the science of brewing. None could match his breadth of knowledge, which was literally worldwide.

As well as his expertise, Nevile's reputation as a champion of the industry was a byword. It was widely known that he had thrown away a knighthood in 1920 by writing to *The Times* opposing the transfer of the Central Control Board to the Home Office.

And on top of everything, he was an extremely imposing personality, his encyclopaedic knowledge emerging in a tremendous voice from a very well-upholstered body. Although he might not be able to overcome the financial conservatism of Whitbread's older directors, in every operational sphere of the company's activities Nevile's word was unchallenged.

Denied the easy solution of a large-scale merger, Nevile redoubled his efforts to turn Whitbread into a modern organization. His first weapon in this formidable quest was information. Nevile was a glutton for facts and, thanks to the typewriter, his files were soon overflowing with it.

Accidents in the brewery; terms for sole agency agreements; policy for supplying bottling agents; press advertising; window-dressing in off-licences; prices for competing beers; the decline of the Stout trade; new standards for bottle sizes and colours; how to improve sales of Special

An advertisement of the 1930s.

Whitbread; notes on a visit to Belgium; infection in the brewery; office cleaning; the 'triple alliance' with Mann's and Truman's; the reorganization of the abroad-coopers' walks (the rounds of Whitbread's tied houses made by its salesmen); reports on hops; a study on rebuilding licensed premises – nothing failed to pass under Nevile's shrewd scrutiny.

Even so, it took him a long time to evolve a new strategy for Whitbread. For several years all that Nevile seemed to be doing was run fast to stay in the same place. But this disguised the foundations of good business practice that he was laying.

Much of his energy in the 1920s was devoted to improving the quality of Whitbread's beer. The introduction of bright beer in London was only the start of a dedicated pursuit of more efficient production methods which, over the course of 20 years, made Whitbread one of the most up-to-date brewers in the country. His pursuit of better standards in Whitbread's public houses was equally persistent and rigorous. So much so that by the end of 1929 he had to take time off to recover from overwork. Typically, his idea of relaxation was a busman's holiday to Tooth's, the brewery his mother's brothers had founded in Australia. Equally typically, he came back full of ideas, including the importation of Australian wine.

But it was a project that he had been considering just before he left England that proved more significant. A couple of years earlier Whitbread had introduced a new strong ale called Double Brown, selling at a premium price of 9d. a bottle, 2d. more than the standard India Pale Ale. Designed as a rival to Guinness, Double Brown was almost a re-creation of Whitbread's original porter, a 'beer of excellent gravity, nourishing, appetizing and refreshing'. It had, according to the advertising blurb, 'a splendid full flavour imparted to it by the fine British Malt and Kentish Hops from which it is brewed and has a splendid sparkling appearance and a beautiful creamy head. It is warming when you are cold, stimulating when you are tired and refreshing when you are hot.' And a four-page publicity brochure was illustrated with a bottle of Double Brown personified as Samuel Whitbread I, over the slogan 'Good for him and good for you, since seventeen hundred and forty-two'.

On 11 November 1929 Nevile dictated some notes on the new beer. They began with an agreement to spend up to £20,000 over twelve months on promotion in London and the Home Counties. The first steps, Nevile thought, should be advertisements in tied houses and off-licences. Special window displays should be encouraged. Press advertising was a possibility, but only in good positions. A strong comparison with Bass, Worthington and Guinness should be made. The memo was evidence of Nevile's growing appreciation of three new facets of business in the modern world: added value, brand names and publicity.

The need to raise the social status of Whitbread's bottled beer and support off-licence sales inspired Nevile to launch an advertising campaign in illustrated weekly magazines of the kind that were read by the comfortably off. He conceived the idea of persuading celebrated people to be photographed dining at well-known restaurants with a bottle of Whitbread on the table instead of wine. The most popular star of the

During the 1930s, Whitbread produced several calendars advertising its main brands of bottled beer.

Double Brown Stout, launched in 1927, used this familiar figure for all its advertising.

WHITBREAD PUBS TODAY
The Bankes Arms Hotel (right) in
Corfe Castle, Dorset, was built by
the Bankes family in the fifteenth
century as a hotel. Owned by the
National Trust, the Bankes Arms
became a Whitbread pub in the late
1960s. Across the road is the
Greyhound Inn, a pub since 1733
and a Strong's house until that
brewery was acquired by Whitbread
in 1968.

Off-licences would sometimes devote whole windows to promoting a single name or brand.

moment was Gertie Lawrence. Afraid of insulting her with a fee, Sydney offered her a cheque for any stage charity she cared to name. To his delight she accepted. So did Ronald Squire, an almost equally famous name.

The only snag was the refusal of famous restaurants to associate themselves with anything as low as beer. Finally one was persuaded to co-operate. Before the advertisement appeared in print, Nevile asked the two renowned thespians to lunch at Chiswell Street. The eagerness with which Harry Whitbread's elder brother Samuel Howard hosted the party was a revelation to the younger directors. Gertie Lawrence charmed everyone, toured the brewery like royalty and was photographed driving a dray, wearing the driver's top hat.

The campaign was a huge success and led to more set-piece advertisements featuring stage and screen personalities.

Nevile decided Whitbread needed a publicity manager and hired a newspaper advertising executive called Hal Douglas Thomson. One of the objectives Thomson was set was raising the status of public houses. He suggested putting fine art into them. Nothing loath, Sydney authorized him to commission four of Britain's most popular Royal Academicians to paint pictures which could be reproduced and hung in all Whitbread's pubs. Sir Alfred Munnings, inevitably, painted the drayhorses.

The value of Whitbread's publicity drive was shown in a slow recovery in sales. It was not before time. They had been languishing around 500,000 barrels ever since the 1931 Economy Budget had increased the tax on beer by 31s. a barrel. Writing in the *House of Whitbread*, the company magazine that he had founded in 1920, Nevile commented: 'It is natural in times such as these that each one of us should consider himself the particular victim who has suffered out of all proportion to the rest of the world. Although it is difficult to appreciate other people's hardships, the beer-drinker at least has the grim satisfaction of knowing that he is contributing more than his full share to the Exchequer.'

Whitbread sought to raise the social standing of its bottled beers with advertisements like these, in which personalities such as the actress Gertrude Lawrence and the actor Ronald Squire (far right) were photographed enjoying a bottle of Whitbread's at a 'quality' restaurant.

Miss Winifred Shotter and Mr. Ralph Lynn enjoying supper at Sovrani's Blue Train Restaurant

POPULAR FAVOURITES AFTER A DANCE

A REFRESHING PICTURE OF MRS. GERTRUDE LAWRENCE AND MR. RONALD SQUIRE

Sir Alfred Munnings's 1937 painting of the North Yard at Chiswell Street.

He continued gloomily: 'A principle of indirect taxation is that it shall be borne by the public. In this instance it is obvious that the consuming public are not in a position to shoulder the whole burden; it is therefore obvious that this unexpected impost will entail heavy losses on the wholesale and retail trade.'

The accuracy of this prophesy was borne out in a fall of 50,000 barrels in Whitbread's production. Profits after tax, however, only declined slightly. It was Whitbread's staff that suffered most from the swingeing increases in tax, so much so that the board made interest-free loans at the end of 1932 to anyone who could not pay the Inland Revenue's latest demands.

Another pressure on the business in the early 1930s came from the report of the Royal Commission, which called for further reductions in licences. Nevile's special advice had not been without influence, as the report recommended improvements to public houses and special hotel and restaurant licences. But Sydney wrote critically:

Although anonymous, with the two figures in silhouette, this advertisement was one of a series that continued the promotion of beer as a socially acceptable drink.

> The recommendations bear the specious stamp of the enlightened reformer, but on a closer examination all hopes of constructive recommendations for legislation are doomed to disappointment. Privileges granted with the one hand are immediately withdrawn with the other, while most of the incentives for public improvements are rendered nugatory by conditions and restrictions worthy of DORA [Defence of the Realm Act] at her worst.

All that Whitbread could oppose to these external constraints were Nevile's endeavours to increase sales. Among them was an attempt to widen the range of products supplied by Whitbread to its retail outlets. An

A Stowell's soda siphon, c. 1920.

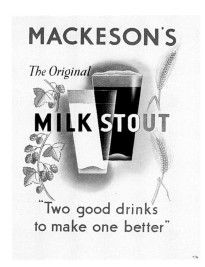

MACKESON'S

The Original

MILK STOUT

"Two good drinks
to make one better"

Above: A Mackeson's Milk Stout
advertisement from the 1930s. Mackeson's
brewery was bought by Whitbead in 1929.

The County Arms, Blaby, was built in 1938.
It is a typical example of 1930s modernist style
and represents a major change in pub
architecture.

extension of the 'tie', in other words. One addition was cider. Sydney wrote to all the leading manufacturers, including Bulmer's, with whom he eventually finalized a deal. He also did his best to develop exports, although attempts to sell Whitbread Pale Ale in the colonies met with mixed results, in spite of direct marketing to every British club from Ahmednagar to Yokohama. An approach to Canada Dry Corporation was even less encouraging.

It was tempting to insist that the Whitbread tied houses only bought wine and spirits from Stowell's, but Nevile resisted the idea. By the standards of the industry, Whitbread gave its tenants remarkable liberty to buy all but their basic beer stocks where they liked. Tenants boasted: 'When you're with Whitbreads you're free.'

Stowell's was fortunately doing well enough on its own, with sales in 1934, for example, of 9,000 barrels of bottled beer, 52,000 gallons of wine and 38,000 gallons of spirits. So, too, was the Improved Public House Company, although more by incorporating some of Whitbread's bigger and more profitable pubs than by building new ones of its own. There was a feeling among Whitbread's tenants that Nevile was creating first and second divisions, with most of the investment going into the premier league. There was truth in the allegation.

The Improved Public House Company, however, was helping Whitbread to raise its profile. It was one reason why in 1937 Whitbread was offered a majority shareholding in Welwyn Restaurants, which gave it the monopoly on beer supplies to Welwyn Garden City's five pubs.

The Kent Breweries, as the combine of Leney, Jude Hanbury and Mackeson were known in Chiswell Street, had also begun to earn their keep once Nevile had ousted the old management and taken control himself. He ran them as a personal fiefdom, using Mackeson's brewery at Hythe as a basic training-ground for management recruits. Among the Hythe brewery's products, incidentally, was a smooth, dark stout flavoured with lactose. To begin with Nevile was unimpressed with this patent product, but then he discovered its quality was being impaired by Customs' restrictions on the use of lactose. Unable to resist the challenge, he used his personal clout to get

WHITBREAD PUBS TODAY

The Uxbridge Arms in Notting Hill, London, has been a Whitbread pub for over a hundred years. There has been an inn on the site since the eighteenth century, although the present building (*left and above left* in 1991 and, *above*, in 1927) dates from the end of the nineteenth century, when the surrounding Hillgate village was built to house the workers constructing the London Underground.

Above: *Bill Whitbread (right) and his father, Harry, at the Mackeson cricket match in 1936.*

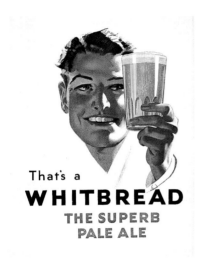

That's a
WHITBREAD
THE SUPERB PALE ALE

Above: *This advertisement for Whitbread's Pale Ale was greatly admired for the quality of its draughtsmanship.*

Whitbread used massive advertisements at London's main railway stations in the 1930s. This one was at Victoria.

the regulations changed, improved the beer and then test-marketed it in Sheffield. To his surprise Mackeson's Milk Stout was a runaway success.

By 1939 Nevile was satisfied that most of his targets had been met. If sales were still a long way from the 1913 peak they were a third higher than seven years before. The technical standards at Chiswell Street and elsewhere were higher than they had ever been and Whitbread's beer was as good if not better than any other on the market. And the Whitbread name had acquired a new lustre. He was 65 years old. There were younger men who could take his place, among them Harry Whitbread's son William and Maurice Martineau's son John, both of them already managing directors. It was time to think about retiring – except that war had been declared against Germany and the younger men were once again departing for the Armed Forces. There was nothing for it but to soldier on.

Nevile had been expecting war for several years, his regular trips to German breweries giving him an early awareness of Hitler's malign influence. Whitbread's air-raid precautions had been drafted since November 1937 and anticipated high explosives, incendiary bombs and gas. Integral to their effectiveness was the company's own fire brigade, which had been founded by Harry Whitbread as long ago as 1892 and in which he had served himself, partly because he liked driving the team and partly to avoid the social invitations his mother Lady Isabella arranged for him.

It had earned its keep on numerous occasions, but the fire brigade's finest hour came on 29 December 1940. Air-raid warnings sounded at ten past six in the evening and during the next five hours hundreds of thousands of explosive and incendiary bombs were dropped on London by the Luftwaffe. The ancient Guildhall, many medieval and Wren churches and acres of offices, shops and homes went up in flames. At one time it was estimated that there were over 4,000 fires burning in the Square Mile.

By good luck no large explosive bombs fell on the brewery, but it was hit by hundreds of incendiaries. Fires started in the hop store and the cooperage, but the fire brigade extinguished them with water from the brewery's reserve tanks. After an hour whole streets around Whitbread were ablaze and the brigade worked from the roof to prevent the flames leaping

The company fire brigade – seen here practising in the South Yard in 1921 – saved the brewery from destruction during the Second World War. Behind the firemen is the ramp that led to the first-floor stables.

Below: Whitbread donated a series of advertisements to answer all sorts of questions provoked by the war.

across the streets on to the brewery buildings. The stables in Garrett Street were ignited and the horses were put into blinkers and moved, two at a time, to the Chiswell Street yard. When the fire was under control, they were led back.

At about half past three the malt tower, on which a steel look-out had been built two years earlier, caught fire and for the first time Whitbread's firefighters had to call in the Auxiliary Fire Service. It was a week before all the smouldering malt was removed.

On the morning of Sunday, 30 December, Whitbread's Chiswell Street brewery stood in a ring of devastation, with only Whitecross Street still open. But the brewery itself was almost undamaged and was back in production four days later.

Below left: The back of the partners' house in the South Yard in 1942 – note that the windows are taped against blast. Despite the best efforts of the fire brigade some buildings were damaged, but production was stopped by enemy action for only four days in the whole war.

Below: The view east from the brewery one week after the great fire raid on 29 December 1940.

Whitbread bottled beers were transported in India and Egypt by a variety of means. Clockwise, from top left, by elephant, on a hand-cart in Karachi, by ox-cart, by camel, by hand (to the mouth), and by motor transport.

In contrast to the First World War, beer production rose rapidly throughout the Second. From only 25 million barrels in 1939, it climbed to 32 million by 1945. At Whitbread, the improvement was even more startling, with a 50 per cent rise to 914,000 barrels, almost up to the record of 989,000 barrels set in 1912.

The increase was in spite of swift leaps in duty, which doubled the price of a pint of beer to a shilling. Supplies of sugar were cut. Then malt. Barley flakes were used to fill the mash tuns, supplemented by oats. Some breweries even used potatoes. The blitz on London made hop-picking more popular than ever, but supplies still fell and the brewers were instructed to cut their hopping rate by 20 per cent which endangered its preservative value. The strength of beer inevitably also fell from an average of around 4 per cent alcohol before the war to about 3 per cent at its end. Some wartime beer was barely alcoholic.

The brewers were also affected by other shortages, of which the most serious was fuel. Only Bass, Worthington and Guinness were classified as national breweries by the Ministry of Food. Whitbread had to accept restrictions on its distribution and 32 of its 200 motor vehicles were requisitioned, the newest and most powerful, of course.

There was also the problem of manpower, or lack of it. A total of 1,176 Whitbread employees served in the three fighting services and the merchant navy, while many hundreds enlisted in the auxiliary forces, the Home Guard and the Women's Land Army. Thirty-eight were killed or died of wounds on active service, with another 16 dead as a result of enemy action.

Publicans suffered as badly as anyone. A total of 565 Whitbread pubs, over 90 per cent of its London licensed houses, were damaged in the blitz, with 29 completely destroyed and another 49 so battered that they had to close. Its bottling-stores, too, were the target of more than 250 attacks. Only the Plymouth depot was so completely blown apart that operations had to be moved. Gray's Inn Road escaped repeatedly.

Like many British companies, Whitbread's decimated workforce contrived an endless series of small miracles, squeezing ever greater production out of ever lessening supplies. One motive was patriotism; another was the absence of anything else to do except work. But at least their efforts were appreciated. Even the *Church Times* admitted that in wartime man needed his cakes and ale and Winston Churchill gave specific instructions for front-line troops to be supplied with beer. A consignment of Whitbread accompanied the prime minister to the Teheran Conference aboard HMS *London*.

When hostilities finally ceased, however, the company, like the country, was exhausted.

A selection of post-Second World War bottles.

The south side of Chiswell Street in 1964. The buildings at the far end of the street have since been demolished. The gateway on the left opens into Whitbread's South Yard.

CHAPTER NINE

A DIRECT DESCENDANT

1945–1971

On 29 June 1948, the chairman of Whitbread wrote a long formal letter to Baring Brothers. It began:

'Gentlemen, I have much pleasure in supplying you with the following information in connection with your Offer for Sale of 204,880 'A' Ordinary Stock Units of £1 each and 204,880 'B' Ordinary Stock Units of 5s. each in this Company'.

More than 200 years after its foundation, Whitbread was finally issuing its shares to the public through the Stock Exchange.

The letter proceeded to outline the history of Whitbread and its current business activities and assets. It revealed that the group employed over 5,000 men and women, that its total assets were valued at £12 million and that it had made a net profit in 1947 of £570,000. In the opinion of the directors, the company had ample working capital and, judging from the results to date, they expected the profits for the year in progress to be at least as good as in the previous year. It explained that, although the offer for sale had been caused by estate duty and high taxation, the management of the business would not be affected. And it disclosed that, pound for pound, the B shares would have 20 times the voting power of the A shares. With 30 per cent of the A shares and 60 per cent of the B shares remaining in the beneficial ownership of the existing directors after the issue, control of Whitbread's future would stay firmly in the hands of the present owners.

It concluded:

I am a direct descendant of the founder, Samuel Whitbread, and my colleague John Edmund Martineau is a great-great-grandson of (the first) John Martineau. It is my earnest wish that the connection between my family and the company may be maintained unbroken and that the very strong sense of tradition engendered by this long connection through generations may also continue hand in hand with

Colonel Bill Whitbread in the 1960s.

the reputation for progressive management of the business, to which our record during the past two centuries entitles us, I think, to lay just claim.

The letter was signed W. H. Whitbread.

Bill Whitbread had been appointed chairman nearly four years earlier, following the death of his uncle Samuel Howard. It was a break with tradition for the job not to go to the senior line of the family, especially as Samuel Howard's son Simon was already on the board. But Nevile, his authority enhanced by the knighthood he had finally received two years earlier, had made it categorically clear that Bill was the only choice.

There was, in fact, no contest. As the heir to Southill, Simon was as detached from the day-to-day running of the brewery as his father had always been. Bill, on the other hand, had been training as a brewer ever since he left Cambridge in 1921, where he had even stayed on for an extra year to study brewing chemistry. He had spent two years learning the trade at Truman Hanbury Buxton and had then worked at Whitbread's Thetford maltings, before moving down to Chiswell Street. There he had served behind the bar, rolled the barrels and looked after the horses, as well as taking an accountancy course, before being made a managing director in 1927. But that is a factually accurate recital with about as much relation to the three-dimensional reality of Bill Whitbread's dominant personality as a shadow puppet to a jack-in-the-box.

The truth was that Bill Whitbread was a fireball. A natural leader who had been captain of almost everything at school, he had become a hunting fanatic at Trinity College, Cambridge. When he was working at Thetford he exercised his horses in the dawn gallops at Newmarket before driving back in time to turn the barley in the malthouse. He was seduced by the

Bill Whitbread on his own horse, Ben Cruachan (right), taking the ditch after Valentine's Brook, first time round in the 1925 Grand National.

What does your glass reveal?
A Whitbread psychological guide.

To the 493 families that still run a butler

a WHITBREAD makes the most of you

Two Whitbread advertisements of the early 1960s.

professional jockeys he met into buying a steeplechaser and for three years he rode almost full time, culminating with two attempts at the Grand National, in both of which he fell, but in both of which he finished.

His racing career was brought to a halt by his engagement to his cousin, Samuel Howard's daughter Joscelyne. At her mother's insistence, Bill dutifully confined his riding to hunting in the winter and polo in the summer. To absorb his surplus energies he sailed, fished and stalked deer in the Highlands.

Anything further from the present-day concept of a managing director would be hard to imagine. But Bill Whitbread found increasing time for the brewery, where his enthusiasm won him the admiration and affection of Sydney Nevile. The two became very close, travelling together around the country and on Nevile's trips to the breweries of Europe.

With the backing of Cecil Lubbock and his father, Harry, as well as Sydney, Bill was poised to take over Whitbread when the Second World War intervened. Aged 39, he trained at the Senior Officers' School on Salisbury Plain and was then posted to the 51st Highlanders. After Dunkirk he was made colonel of the new Reconnaissance Corps formed in anticipation of an eventual return to Europe. Bill's country skills and flying experience, it was said, made him a natural scout. He took part in the invasion of Europe and entered Brussels with the liberation forces, where he personally repossessed Whitbread's bottling-depot on the Avenue de Jubilée. He was involved in the retreat from Arnhem and then toured reconnaissance regiments in Palestine, Greece and Italy.

The death of Samuel Howard sucked him back to the UK to take over the family business. He found it in dire straits. Although production was at near-record levels, the plant and transport were on their last legs and the pubs Whitbread supplied were battered and worn. The only solution was massive and immediate investment.

The major shareholders, however, were in no position to provide it. Samuel Howard's death had been preceded by that of Frank in 1941 and was

A characteristic advertisement of the 1950s.

Now she knows...

the best of the light ales is a WHITBREAD

BOTTLED ONLY BY WHITBREADS

111

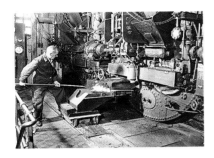

Stoking a boiler at the Chiswell Street brewery in the 1940s.

Loading barrels on to a dray for local delivery. The North Yard at Chiswell Street was the storage and distribution side of the brewery; the beer was brewed on the south side.

followed by Harry Whitbread's in 1947. Maurice Martineau had died in 1943.

Bluntly, Bill Whitbread informed the existing shareholders that they had two choices. One was to agree to Whitbread becoming a public company. The second was to see it sold or run down. The Articles of Association required 100 per cent acceptance of his proposals. The last to concede was a reluctant lieutenant-commander. Bill dosed himself with milk and olive oil and drank the recalcitrant into concurrence.

The money raised, the new chairman set about putting it to work. One of his first actions was to build a new management team. Cecil Lubbock had retired and Sydney Nevile was recovering from a minor operation that he had put off for 25 years. Nevile had also got married two years earlier, at the age of 72. He was not a man to retire, but his role at Whitbread in the future would be advisory.

Jack Martineau had returned from the RAF with the rank of wing-commander and took charge of Chiswell Street. A classics scholar and good with figures, Martineau was a competent manager but his chilly demeanour mirrored a negative approach to risk.

'Colonel' Bill, as he had become known throughout Whitbread, needed a much more positive personality to act as his chief of staff. His direct, not to say brusque, manner required a resilient and ameliorating foil who would temper the wind of his passing. He knew just the man for the job. Ten years younger than the chairman, Alex Bennett was the youthful graduate to whom Sydney Nevile had offered a year's unpaid training. He had accepted and had been sent to the Hythe Brewery, where he had earned the gratitude of the head brewer by sorting out his hopelessly muddled Rest return. Nevile had been impressed enough to relent and employ him as an assistant abroad-cooper at Chiswell Street on £100 a year.

Bennett had distinguished himself throughout the war as an extremely able organizer from the moment he led his Territorial Army platoon to sandbag the Old Bailey to his final posting on Field Marshal Montgomery's staff. His military career included planning the D-Day landings and acting as Army liaison with the explosive personalities at Bomber Command. Calm, cheerful and competent, within two years of returning to Whitbread Bennett was a managing director.

The first few years after the war were devoted to restoring Whitbread's operations in the face of considerable hardship. Britain had acquired debts of £3 billion waging war with Hitler's Germany, had allowed its domestic capital to fall by as much again and had used up another £1 billion of its overseas investments. Exports were down by two-thirds. The United States brought its lend-lease agreements to an abrupt halt on the defeat of Japan and, although North American loans were secured, it was only on the condition that the pound should be restored to full convertibility. The result was the first post-war sterling crisis.

The desire for a welfare state for all had swept the Labour Party into power but the cost of rebuilding the country's economy would have been just as great under the Conservatives. Either way, personal and corporate taxes had to remain high and resources had to be rationed.

And as if all this was not enough, the winter of 1946/7 saw the worst blizzards and the greatest freeze for a century. It was not until the early 1950s that Whitbread could raise its eyes from immediate concerns and look at the wider horizon. What it found was a brewing industry under greater threat than ever before.

The underlying reason was the rise in property values. As business began to pick up, the value of shops and offices, which during the war had collapsed, recovered, with the shortages caused by war damage exacerbating demand. Rents rose dramatically, as did capital values. The development boom did not get fully into its stride until building restrictions were removed in 1954, but long before then astute entrepreneurs like Charles Clore and Maxwell Joseph had grasped the potential value of property assets owned by many old-established businesses. Brewers were especially ripe with their strings of public houses, many on High Street sites, and their large brewery premises, once on the edge of town but now, due to the spread of cities, often all but in the centre.

Whitbread was a prime target. Clore made several approaches. Bill Whitbread was not interested, to the extent of being 'out' when the developer called. Other family breweries were not so determined and a number in London and the bigger provincial cities were snapped up by acquisitive companies alive to their dormant asset values, among them other more aggressive brewers. Brewers in smaller towns, however, offered slimmer pickings to the property developers and had time to prepare their defences. Many turned to Whitbread for help.

Whitbread was highly regarded throughout the UK brewing industry for two reasons. One was its reputation for technical excellence, especially for the manufacture of chilled and filtered beers which dated from the purchase of Forest Hill Brewery and had been perfected by Carl Wootton.

The other was Colonel Bill's own status. He was already well known as an up-and-coming member of the 'beerage', as the media irreverently called the great brewing families. But in 1953 he had become an industry hero when, as chairman of the Brewers' Society, he had stalled the Licensed (Amendment) (Tied Houses) Bill, under which Geoffrey Bing QC proposed to nationalize public houses on all new housing estates.

Below left: In the hop-gardens, manuring, stringing, spraying and hoeing go on all the year round until early September when the hops are ready for picking. The strings are supported 15–20 feet above the ground, so maintenance is carried out on stilts.

Below: In the 1950s the cooperage at Chiswell Street was still producing hundreds of new casks each year and repairing many more. The 108-gallon butts were no longer made but barrels (36 gallons), kilderkins (18 gallons), firkins (9 gallons) and pins (4½ gallons) were still in regular use.

These pages: Between 1961 and 1971 Whitbread merged with 23 other smaller breweries, listed opposite.

Whitbread found itself being all but begged to buy strategic minority shareholdings in regional breweries all over the UK. As these deals invariably included a commitment to stock Whitbread beer, the company had no hesitation in accepting. Within a short time Colonel Bill and Alex Bennett were on the boards of a dozen local breweries.

This defensive arrangement satisfied everyone until the arrival in the UK of E. P. Taylor, the owner of Canadian Breweries. An aggressive colonial who had made a vast fortune selling bootleg beer to prohibitionist America, Eddie Taylor bought the Hope and Anchor Brewery of Sheffield and used the company as his base for an insatiable programme of raids on other provincial companies. His technique was to slap a bid on the table at his first visit. It shocked the sleepy, self-satisfied world of old-fashioned English country breweries to the soles of their brogue-clad feet.

Inevitably, larger British brewers were tempted into counter-attacks and Taylor's offers began to be contested. Colonel Bill met the Canadian just after the latter had lost a closely contested battle for two Bristol breweries to Courage. Furiously, Taylor warned him: 'Unless you do something about your associated companies, I'll take them all!'

The threat was clearly serious and was reinforced by a renewed stream of requests from smaller breweries for Whitbread to act as a 'white knight' by taking minority shareholdings. Responding meant raising capital. A share issue was out of the question. It had been hard enough persuading the old shareholders to give up 25 per cent of their equity. The answer was the formation of the Whitbread Investment Company, with its initial portfolio the minority stakes in the associated breweries. From then on this trust company, in which Whitbread held 49 per cent, became a vehicle for investments in breweries and for raising capital with which to buy them.

The step from protector to proprietor was inevitable, if only because of the pressure from other major brewers. Bill Whitbread resisted until 1961. But then Alex Bennett received a telephone call from Charrington to ask if Whitbread would accept an offer the rival group was about to make for Tennant's of Sheffield, one of the companies under the Whitbread

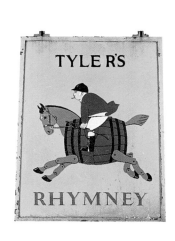

WHITBREAD MERGERS 1961–71

1961	Tennant Bros John R. Fielder & Son	1967	Evan Evans, Bevan Archibald Campbell, Hope & King Threlfalls Chesters Isaac Tucker & Co. Fremlins
1962	Norman & Pring Flowers Breweries Starkey Knight & Ford		
1963	West Country Brewery Holdings J. Nimmo & Son	1968	Cobb & Co. Bentley's Yorkshire Breweries Richard Whitaker & Sons John Young & Co. Combined Breweries (Holdings) Strong & Co. of Romsey
1964	Dutton's Blackburn Brewery		
1965	E. Lacon & Co.		
1966	Rhymney Breweries James Thompson & Co.	1971	Brickwoods

'umbrella', as the press called its investment policy. Bennett summoned Bill Whitbread from a Scottish moor to attend the crucial Tennant's board meeting. At the meeting, Whitbread made a counter-offer. Then he and Bennett withdrew to the potting shed in the chairman's garden while the other directors decided to accept.

Other takeover deals followed. Some were less formal. Colonel Bill found Mr Ford of Starkey Knight & Ford waiting for him on the steps of the brewery in Bridgwater. 'Shall we talk in your office?' Whitbread asked. 'I have no office,' the old man replied. 'I do all my business on these steps. Always have. Now, how much?'

Over the next ten years Whitbread absorbed more than a score of regional breweries, including Flowers of Luton, Dutton's of Blackburn, Lacon's of Great Yarmouth, Archibald Campbell, Hope & King of Edinburgh, Threlfalls of Liverpool, Evan Evans, Bevan of Neath, Fremlins of Maidstone, Bentley's Yorkshire Breweries, Strong & Co of Romsey, Brickwoods of Portsmouth and West Country Breweries. In almost every case the mergers took place by invitation.

Below: Dutton's brewery in Blackburn in the 1880s. The brewery merged with Whitbread in 1964.

WHITBREAD PUBS TODAY

The Royal Oak at Langstone was reputed to have been a smugglers' haunt, with a secret passage connecting it to Langstone Mill. The pub dates back to 1550 when it was one of three cottages. Legend has it that the pub is haunted by the ghost of a small child.

Most of its new acquisitions, as Whitbread found out the hard way, had poor management and vestigial financial controls. Integrating them put a tremendous strain on their new owner. Only too often, the brewing operations were old-fashioned and unreliable. Although customers were fiercely loyal to their local brews, many could only be described as an acquired taste. One of the snags of traditional beer had always been its variability, as Whitbread had known to its cost in the past. There were exceptions, like Tennant's Gold Label barley wine, first brewed in 1951 and soon in the *Guinness Book of Records* as the strongest regularly brewed nationally distributed beer. But not many. Bringing its new subsidiaries into the twentieth century was a huge challenge.

Whitbread did its best, seconding skilled men from Chiswell Street to archaic breweries across the land. But it wasn't long before reality intruded. Progressively, local breweries were closed and their employees made redundant. Bill Whitbread revealed in his statement to shareholders in 1971 that in the previous ten years the group had closed 15 breweries, 24 bottling-plants and 54 distribution depots. 'These are formidable figures, not only as regards planning but in dealing with those employed so that the least unhappiness and disruption of life is caused.'

But he also disclosed that Whitbread still retained ten of the breweries it had acquired, all of which had been improved and enlarged. This was enough to justify Whitbread's professed commitment to local beers, although many had vanished or were being made elsewhere, which tended to reduce them to labels. In their place Whitbread provided its own range, which included Whitbread Pale Ale and Mackeson, beginning to become almost as well known as Guinness thanks to sustained and effective advertising. The Mackeson slogan: 'It looks good. It tastes good. And by Golly it does you good!' delivered in the rich accent of Sir Bernard, later Lord Miles, the founder of the Mermaid Theatre, had become a national catch-phrase.

Other additions to the range included Heineken lager, under licence from Holland, and Whitbread Tankard.

Colonel Bill had recognized that a taste for lager was beginning to develop in the UK in the early 1960s. He had decided that importing a genuine Continental lager was a better idea than manufacturing a British version, unlike Guinness, which was introducing Harp, or Allied Breweries, which produced Skol. He had instead talked first to the de Spoelbergh family, who owned the Belgian brewery Artois, and then, when these discussions failed to progress, approached Heineken. The initial agreement with Heineken envisaged a jointly owned lager brewery in the UK once sales reached 50,000 barrels a year, but in the event Whitbread decided full ownership was a better bet. By 1969 Heineken was being brewed under licence at Luton, with a Dutch brewer on site to ensure quality control.

A special lower-gravity lager was brewed to take advantage of favourable rates of excise duty. Heineken originally had doubts about this, as their principal product everywhere else in the world was stronger. They were persuaded by Whitbread's promise that sales of the lower gravity lager would

Sir Albert Richardson (left) and Sydney Nevile at the opening of the Bull's Head, Guildford, newly built by Whitbread in 1958.

Canned beers first appeared in the 1930s. This can of Mackeson stout was produced in the 1950s.

Beer mats provided a cheap and easily distributable form of advertising for use in pubs.

The White Knight pub in Crawley is typical of the 1960s style of architecture.

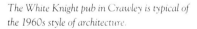

be much larger. Within two years the claim had been substantiated, with Heineken holding 20 per cent of the UK lager market.

Artois, not surprisingly, showed signs of regret that it had not seized this opportunity itself. Whitbread agreed to restrict sales of high-gravity Heineken, which Whitbread was importing but was finding was being confused with its weaker, own-brewed version, in favour of Stella Artois. The decision to sell Stella Artois as Whitbread's premium lager proved successful and in due course the Belgian lager became the leading high-gravity lager in the UK, like Heineken manufactured by Whitbread under licence.

Tankard, which was launched in 1957, was Whitbread's first container beer. Pioneered on a commercial scale by Watney's as Red Barrel and by Flowers Brewery as Flowers Keg, this was a new system of managing and dispensing beer. It provided public houses with metal kegs or casks containing clear filtered beer which had been made to sparkle with natural fermentation gas. All the publican had to do was connect the casks to a transparent plastic pipe and raise the carbonated beer to his bar with a small gas-powered pump. The method eliminated time-consuming cellar management, as well as the risk of contamination from air or dirt, and guaranteed that the beer would reach the customer's glass in exactly the condition it had left the brewery. A further refinement was to refrigerate the pipeline near the bar, so that the beer was served at a predetermined temperature regardless of the warmth of the cask. By 1971 container beers accounted for more than 50 per cent of the total beer market in England and Wales. Not all customers were enthusiastic, as the vigorous and influential Campaign for Real Ale testified. But brewers and publicans loved them.

The spate of takeovers had enormously expanded Whitbread's tied estate. The chairman told shareholders in his 1971 statement that shortly after the war, only 20 per cent of Whitbread's trade had been tied. Now the figure was nearly 60 per cent, although this was still considerably less than its major competitors. What this statement concealed was just how many pubs and off-licences the group had come to own – about 9,000 out of a total of 90,000 in the whole country. The rationalization of the industry had reached the point where six companies, Allied Breweries, Bass

The Royal Visit of 1962, painted by Terence Cuneo. On the right can be seen the Queen, the Queen Mother, Bill Whitbread and other members of the Board.

Charrington, Courage, Scottish & Newcastle, Watneys and Whitbread, controlled an estimated 80 per cent of all retail beer sales.

Whitbread was aware that such a change in the industry must affect the relationship between brewers and publicans. It was doing its best to define this relationship. 'Whitbread tenants are regarded as independent businessmen working in partnership with us to provide a high standard of service to the public and to obtain the maximum return on capital invested for us both,' Bill Whitbread told shareholders. During 1971 the company reached agreement with the National Federation of Licensed Victuallers and the London Central Board of Licensed House Managers for all its new tenants to buy their beer at free trade prices and gave all its existing tenants the option to do the same. From October all tenants could improve their security of tenure by applying for a three-year agreement.

The company did not, however, admit that the concentration of pub ownership was bad. Only the year before, indeed, the Monopolies and Mergers Commission had produced a nil report, after spending two and a half years investigating the industry, at a great cost in time and effort to the brewers. In addition, Whitbread had twice been summoned before the Prices and Incomes Board. 'There has been a general interference in industry and a desire to pry into other people's affairs,' Bill Whitbread remarked acidly. He made no secret of his delight that the Tories had just won the general election and that controls on the price of beer were being lifted.

He was even more pleased to report that Whitbread's new brewery in Luton had opened with a capacity of over one million barrels a year. Building a new brewery had fulfilled one of his lifetime ambitions. 'We are having a constant stream of visitors from abroad who wish to see it. This is a slight embarrassment in our first summer of full production,' he commented, unwittingly echoing Joseph Delafield's remark about Chiswell Street nearly two centuries earlier.

Finally, Bill Whitbread announced that he had decided to retire. He had been chairman for 27 years, during which Whitbread's profits after tax had risen from £300,000 to nearly £10 million and its assets from less than £9 million to more than £200 million. It was a high point on which to go.

This advertisement came out shortly after decimalization was introduced in 1971.

What indulgences can 8p buy you nowadays?

Lauter tuns at Salmesbury.

CHAPTER TEN

THERE'S A TERRIFIC DRAUGHT. . .

1971–1985

Perhaps the most appropriate word to describe the history of Whitbread over the last 21 years is 'metamorphosis'. The pace of change during the period has been so rapid and its nature so fundamental that it is hardly an exaggeration to say that the group has been born again.

For that matter, the whole of the British economy could be said to have been transformed by a new industrial revolution. The impact of modern technology on production costs has brought a cornucopia of conveniences within the reach of many. Colour television and package holidays have changed the way we spend our leisure time and altered our eating and drinking habits. Car ownership and refrigerators have led to convenience foods and out-of-town supermarkets. In not much more than a generation the historic domination of demand by supply has given way to a consumer society in which the customer rules, with consequences that are only just beginning to be appreciated.

The effect on the drinks industry has been as profound as anywhere else. It has forced public houses to change their ways and widen their appeal. And it has irrevocably shifted the emphasis of the business from making to selling.

The concentration of the brewing industry was an essential precursor to this change. As far back as 1948 Bill Whitbread had articulated the inevitability of this process in the words: 'If we don't integrate, we will disintegrate.' But it was his successors who grasped that the next stage in the evolutionary process was the transfer of power from the producer to the retailer.

The staggering growth of Whitbread's traditional business in the 1960s may have overshadowed them, but the seeds of change were already planted when Colonel Bill retired.

Alex Bennett, chairman of Whitbread from 1971 to 1978.

One embryo was its wines and spirits business, which by then embraced retailers Threshers and Mackies and investments in Standfast whisky and Squires gin, as well as wholesalers Stowells of Chelsea.

Another was Whitbread International, formed in 1967 to take over the group's forays overseas, where Whitbread aimed to increase earnings to a third of total trading profits.

A third was a new soft-drinks division incorporating three mineral-water companies, including Rawlings and R. White & Sons, known for its lemonade, and Whitbread's Coca-Cola franchise for central England.

A fourth was restaurants and hotels. In 1971 Whitbread had just bought 100 per cent of Severnside Hotels from Trust Houses and had formed a joint company called Whitly Inns with J. Lyons. It was also operating over a hundred restaurants.

And finally there was Whitbread Trafalgar Properties, a partnership with Trafalgar House Investments to exploit the group's gigantic property portfolio. Well over a hundred of the juicier titbits had been selected for redevelopment, of which the richest was Chiswell Street itself.

But although these new divisions and companies sounded good on paper, to begin with they were not much more than names on paper. The immediate truth was that Whitbread had dangerously outgrown its still essentially personal management. For more than a quarter of a century, Bill Whitbread had run his family business with the same dash and flair that had characterized his steeplechasing. Combined with his deep knowledge of brewing and his talent for leadership, his personal talents had almost single-handedly turned Whitbread into one of the giants of the industry. It was an extraordinary achievement.

The task of digesting its huge meal, however, required a much more formal and disciplined approach. Already some of its ventures were looking a little ragged. For the first time, too, labour relations were deteriorating and their repair was going to take more than a personal plea from the

Threshers was acquired as part of Flowers Breweries in 1962. It has become Whitbread's main off-licence chain, with over 1,000 branches. Some stores now sell food as well as a wide variety of drinks. This store in Leominster, Herefordshire, was bought by Threshers in 1989.

BEFORE   AFTER

Heineken. Refreshes the parts other beers cannot reach.

chairman. In fact, labour relations had started fraying some time before
Colonel Bill stood down. The harmful progress the unions were making in
the business stemmed in no small way from his unwillingness to allow
strikes. When Whitbread finally faced up to the TGWU at Luton, Robin
Farrington, the manager in the firing line, spent almost as much time in the
chairman's office reassuring him that they were doing the right thing as he
spent negotiating with the union.

The vacuum left by Bill Whitbread's retirement was filled at the top by
Alex Bennett, who took over as chairman. One of his first acts was to
announce the creation of an executive committee to run Whitbread on a
day-to-day basis. The committee had nine members. Among them were
Charles Tidbury and Farrington.

Tidbury had joined Whitbread in 1953 at the age of 26. He had been
commissioned in the King's Royal Rifle Corps and had spent two years in
Palestine, after which he had learned Russian and worked at 'something to
do with the atom bomb' at GCHQ. But a subsequent posting had left him
languishing in Germany. Tidbury had gone sailing with Bill Whitbread, to
whom he was related by marriage, and had confessed his frustration.
Whitbread had offered him a job and Tidbury had served his two-year
apprenticeship at Hythe and Chiswell Street. Energetic and decisive, he
had made his mark on the technical front by analysing Whitbread's need for
a high-quality bitter beer and on the marketing side selling Mackeson to
small breweries. When Alex Bennett fell ill for a time in the late 1950s, it
was Tidbury who filled the breach. By 1959 he was a managing director.

Robin Farrington had joined Whitbread five years later. He had been in
Palestine with Tidbury and, after Cambridge, had worked for a Lloyd's
broking firm, running its reinsurance office in Switzerland, where his fluent
German and French stood him in good stead. Offered a job at Whitbread,
he had been among the first management recruits to query his prospects for
a top job in what he perceived as still essentially a family business.
Clear-thinking and firm-minded, Farrington drafted the trading agreements
with all the 'umbrella' companies and was chairman of the planning and
rationalization committee which handled their integration when they were
eventually taken over by Whitbread.

Farrington could not avoid being intimately aware of the pressures that
Whitbread's stream of takeovers was building up. He was not alone. When

*One of the first Heineken advertisements,
brought out in 1974. Retaining its wit and
appeal over 20 years, it has been one of the
most durable advertising campaigns ever.*

*Charles (later Sir Charles) Tidbury, chairman
from 1978 until 1984, was one of the key
managers of change in Whitbread.*

Strangeways brewery, Manchester, where Boddingtons Bitter is brewed.

The hop room in Strangeways. Hops of different varieties and years are stored here, to be used in varying quantities, depending on the flavour required.

Colonel Bill agreed to buy the Welsh brewery Evan Evans, Bevan on the train from Swansea, forcing Whitbread to borrow £6 million from Barclays Bank, there was more than a little concern in Chiswell Street.

Tidbury's thinking had been revolutionized by a course at INSEAD in 1962. This had introduced him to the concept of marketing. He became an avid reader of management gurus like Peter Drucker and Robert Heller, with John Adair's *Training for Decisions* a virtual bible. His studies made him powerfully aware of Whitbread's strengths and weaknesses. On the one hand he realized the value of the company's fundamental commitment to quality. But he also learned that all great businesses had to accept change.

The new management team's progress was hampered as much by the Labour Government's attempts to control industry as by the economic tribulations of the UK. As chairman, Bennett complained bitterly about the time senior management spent reporting to the Price Commission and there were renewed threats of nationalization. Whitbread Trafalgar Properties counted itself lucky to have been granted the last substantial office development permit for Chiswell Street before total restriction came into force at the end of 1973.

The combination of the Price Code, part of the Government's prices and incomes policy, and inflation inevitably cut into profit margins. Earnings dipped sharply in 1974. However, they recovered to a new record of £30 million in 1975, reflecting increased sales of beer, especially draught bitter and lager, for which demand had flourished since it was launched on draught in 1969, stimulated by the slogans: 'There's A Terrific Draught Blowing Your Way' and, since 1974: 'Heineken Refreshes The Parts Other Beers Cannot Reach'. The ten millionth barrel of Heineken was brewed in 1976. By then most of Whitbread's beer was being produced at Luton and at Salmesbury, where a second new brewery had been completed four years earlier. A third, at Magor in South Wales, came on stream in 1979, by which time lager accounted for 33 per cent of the UK beer market. The modernization programme had not, however, applied to Chiswell Street, where brewing had finally ceased in 1976 after two and a quarter centuries.

The rest of Whitbread's beer business had by then been brought up to date, including the modernization of its distribution network with new vehicles and handling systems. Ten new depots had been built and existing

The Exchange brewery on the river Don in Sheffield was acquired from Tennant Bros in 1961.

Hop room, Strangeways brewery.

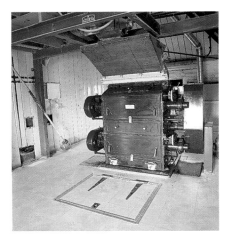

Malt mill, Cheltenham.

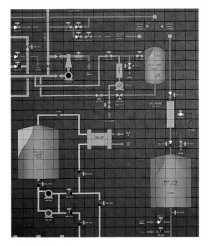

Lauter tun CIP (cleaning in place) panel, Salmesbury.

The principles of brewing beer may have remained unchanged from 250 years ago, but the process is no longer a mystery. Instead, Whitbread's present-day breweries make beer with scientific precision in hygienic conditions. With its stainless-steel containers and its electronic controls, beer production today appears an anonymous, high-tech process compared with the past.

Coppers, Exchange brewery, Sheffield.

Yeast room, Cheltenham.

Barrels, Strangeways brewery, Manchester.

Filtration plant sight glass, Salmesbury.

Mash tun-room, Cheltenham.

Canning line, Magor (the moving cans are the blurred lines to the right of the picture).

Whitbread 'big-head' Trophy Bitter was a popular beer in the 1970s and was promoted through a series of strong advertisements (right). Whitbread Tankard (below) was a premium brand for the company.

This is one of a series of advertisements for Flowers Bitter that punned on the name.

ones improved and extended. Whitbread also pressed ahead with a detailed survey of its licensed houses. Many were earmarked for sale. Galloping inflation meant that rents had to be raised. Tenants were not enthusiastic. They, too, were being squeezed. But most of them accepted Whitbread's terms, however reluctantly. Along with higher rents, however, came improvements.

A long hot summer in 1977 stretched Whitbread's production capacity to the limit, but although profits rose again Bennett reported that they were still not keeping pace with the rise in the Retail Price Index. In real terms, like the rest of British industry, Whitbread's margins were contracting.

The difficulty of making real money in the UK and the growing threat to the 'tie' stimulated efforts to become less reliant on beer and to diversify abroad.

The value of overseas earnings had been highlighted by tax concessions designed to stimulate exports. In theory, Whitbread was well placed to expand abroad, with its long tradition of exporting beer to the colonies and its well-established position in Belgium, where it owned a small brewery as well as a new bottling-plant. Its international reputation was also high, with foreign brewing companies eager to buy its technical know-how.

But past efforts to brew beer abroad had not been anything to write home about, as Robin Farrington knew better than anyone. Plans to build a brewery in the Western Region of Nigeria had collapsed at the last minute – Taylor Woodrow had already cleared the site – due to a coup in the West African country which had resulted in all the people Whitbread was dealing with being either killed or imprisoned, and had been replaced by a similar venture in South Africa in partnership with Heineken and Anton Rupert of Rembrandt. This investment came up against South African Breweries' effective monopoly and was looking extremely vulnerable when Farrington learned that the market leader was short of capacity. It was a piece of market intelligence that enabled Whitbread to sell out to South African Breweries at something near break-even point.

Efforts were made to sell more Whitbread beer to other parts of the Commonwealth. Jamaica and Trinidad began brewing Mackeson under licence in 1973 and the Leopard Brewery in New Zealand launched Whitbread Premium Draught in 1975.

Tidbury and Farrington, however, thought that Europe looked more attractive. Once again hopes flattered only to deceive. Whitbread came close to acquiring France's largest brewing company, Société Européenne de Brasseries, only to withdraw when the subtleties of its ownership by the Alsatian financier René Hinzelin became clear. Then Heineken suggested a joint rescue of Birra Dreher, which held 22 per cent of the Italian beer market but was crumbling under union pressure. Farrington and Jap Stap, Heineken's finance director and an ex-Olympic dinghy sailor, were sent to negotiate the deal.

They looked at the business and made three demands. The first was to the Italian Government for the removal of price control on beer. The second, to the consortium of 25 banks propping up the company, was for long-term finance at a fixed interest rate of 8.5 per cent, well below the market rate of 20 per cent. The third, to the Dreher shareholders, was that they hand over the business for nothing. To emphasize their negotiating position at the crucial meeting with the banks, Farrington and Stap sat on either side of Professor Cassella, Milan's leading bankruptcy lawyer, with their passports and airline tickets out of the country prominant on the table. All three demands were met.

Used to inspiring terror in Italian managers, the union bosses were nonplussed by similarly uncompromising tactics as Farrington closed two of Dreher's five breweries. However, after 18 months managing the business, Farrington reported that Dreher remained undercapitalized and Whitbread sold out its stake to Heineken, which was already benefiting from the Italian company brewing lager under licence.

It was a decision which threw a strain on the link between Whitbread and Heineken. Ray van Schaik, later chairman of the executive board of Heineken, subsequently remarked to Farrington that if Whitbread had stayed in Dreher, it might have led to other joint ventures which could have totally altered the long-term relationship between the two brewing giants.

Meanwhile, however, Farrington negotiated the joint purchase with Artois of a Belgian ale brewery called Martinas, into which Whitbread moved its Belgian beer production, closing its own brewery and doubling its profits overnight.

Earlier, Farrington had headed a strategic study which concluded that lager sales in the UK would continue to grow and that it would be dangerous for Whitbread to become too dependent on imported brands, while sales of ale in Europe would never make similar headway. Merger talks with Artois were begun, foundering on the objections not of Whitbread but of Artois family shareholders.

Whitbread also took a fresh look at the UK lager market and concluded there was room for at least two other brands, a lower-gravity product and a Pils-type superstrength brew.

The first, Heldenbrau, it produced itself, while Farrington was instructed to look for a Bavarian lager with a good name and under-utilized assets.

A search of more than 2,000 Bavarian breweries resulted in the acquisition of the Kaltenberg brand name from Prince Luitpold von Bayern, a direct descendant of King Ludwig II. Prince Luitpold, who brewed Kaltenberg in his castle, was young and enthusiastic. Whitbread helped him to buy a second brewery in Bavaria.

Other European investments included the old-established German wine-producer Langenbach in Worms. But an honest assessment of

Whitbread lorries are painted with the liveries of key brands – a common method of advertising. This one, with driver Brian Harris, is at the Whitbread Centre at Hedge End, a village in Hampshire.

Heldenbrau and Kaltenberg, two lagers brewed in the UK by Whitbread. Heldenbrau was a new creation, while Kaltenberg was an acquisition.

Whitbread began Pizza Hut (UK) as a joint venture with PepsiCo in 1982. It has grown into one of the great success stories of the modern group.

Beefeater 'Mr Men' menus are very popular with children. Beefeater has been another growth area for Whitbread in the 1980s.

Whitbread's European activities had to conclude that the company was not willing to invest on the scale needed to exploit the potential of its Continental businesses.

That left North America. Visits to the United States between the wars by Nevile, Bill Whitbread, Jack Martineau and others had resulted in a fairly firm consensus that British beer was not to American taste. Neither exporting nor licensing Whitbread looked as though it would be profitable. Still, some beer was sent to the East Coast and in 1975 exports began to Los Angeles, although it wasn't long before Whitbread handed over marketing to a small American agency called All Brand Importers, in which it subsequently acquired a 49 per cent stake.

The expansion of Whitbread's wines and spirits division in the States followed the purchase in 1975 of Long John International, a Scottish distiller whose brands included Laphroaig whisky, Plymouth gin and Seagers gin. The acquisition of Long John reflected the belief that Whitbread should acquire its own brands of spirits, particularly Scotch whisky. A significant percentage of Long John's production was for export and the company provided a vehicle with which to take over Highland Distillers Corporation of California a few years later. Further acquisitions helped Whitbread's wines and spirits division to enlarge its market share abroad as well as in the UK.

Wines and spirits were, of course, an important part of Whitbread's turnover. Large quantities were sold through its public houses and off-licences. Although Colonel Bill pretended to lack of interest in wines and spirits, this did not stop him bargaining fiercely with the Distillers Company for greater discounts for quantity purchases. One row culminated in Whitbread founding the Squires Gin consortium in 1957, to which some 80 brewers subscribed and which led to Squires becoming the second largest gin brand in the UK after Gordons. As demand for wine and spirits grew, investments were made in William Grant, the Wine Traders' Consortium and, with Allied Breweries, in J. R. Phillips, an agency specializing in spirits and liqueur brands. Stowells of Chelsea was also reorganized and given a national identity.

Considerable benefits also accrued from the partnership with Trafalgar House, with the redevelopment of Chiswell Street the largest single project. It took six years to get planning permission, but in 1976 the brewery buildings on the two acres south of the porter tun-room were demolished and two office blocks with a total floor space of 400,000 square feet built on the site and let, and later sold, to BP.

The lower part of the porter tun-room was turned into an exhibition hall for the 272-foot-long Overlord Embroidery, which commemorated the invasion of Normandy in 1944 and had taken the Royal School of Needlework five years to complete. Other parts of the brewery were rebuilt as banqueting and reception rooms, conference centres and offices for Whitbread's senior management.

On the north side of Chiswell Street a two-acre redevelopment included shops, stores and a supermarket, a squash club and a 'planning gain' of 138 council flats for Islington. The whole development took another six years,

The Monkey Puzzle Beefeater restaurant in Chessington was purpose-built in 1989 with a Travel Inn added a year later. It exemplifies how Beefeater continues to evolve, satisfying changing customer demand.

won a heritage award and earned Whitbread £25 million. Its completion was one of the highlights of Charles Tidbury's period as chairman of Whitbread, which had begun at the beginning of 1978.

Reporting on 1982, Tidbury informed shareholders that the group's turnover had exceeded £1 billion for the first time. Assets, too, were over this impressive figure, reflecting the great rise in the value of property.

It had been another difficult year, of course, with the UK still struggling to emerge from the recession that accompanied Margaret Thatcher's determined stand against inflation. But the lager market had revived and the launch of Stowells Wine Box had been a spectacular success.

Tidbury drew particular attention to new opportunities for Whitbread to invest in the provision of food. As well as encouraging its publicans to diversify into catering, Whitbread was building up an impressive chain of Beefeater Steak Houses, was experimenting with other restaurant concepts such as Roast-Inns and Hungry Fishermen, and had just started a joint venture with PepsiCo called Pizza Hut (UK).

Whitbread's international trade had also been expanded with the acquisition in the USA of Julius Wile, a highly regarded wine-importer, and Fleischmann, a substantial producer of spirits.

Inside, the Monkey Puzzle lives up to its name, with tables in a variety of nooks and crannies.

131

Sam Whitbread, the founder's great-great-great-great-grandson, became chairman in 1984.

The Queen Mother and Bill Whitbread at the Whitbread Trial Chase, Ascot, in 1972.

Whitbread produce a range of items for sponsored events including the Round-the-World Yacht Race.

Tidbury also reported that Anthony Simonds-Gooding had taken over from him as group managing director. Simonds-Gooding had been recruited by Alex Bennett as marketing director nine years earlier and had made a noticeable contribution to the new emphasis on retailing. Robin Farrington became a vice-chairman, as did Martin Findlay. Findlay remained personnel director, which reflected the importance that industrial relations had assumed. Although Tidbury could tell shareholders that these had been good throughout the year, communications with employees still needed improving and relations with the workforce at Luton was a running sore which never healed. Hard as people like Findlay tried, the Luton brewery continued to suffer, as they saw it, from mouth-to-mouth contagion from the motor unions. As a result, the brewery was closed in the middle of 1984.

By then Tidbury had retired, his place as chairman taken by Simon Whitbread's son Samuel Charles, the great-great-great-great-grandson of the founder. The new chairman revealed that the closure of the Luton brewery had meant the loss of 275 jobs, but that 178 had found new ones, 15 had started their own businesses, six had taken early retirement, five had moved away and one had been retrained. Great credit for this was due to FOCUS, an organization owned jointly by Whitbread and the London Chamber of Commerce and Industry, which had been set up to cope with compulsory redundancies in industry in the UK. And, in spite of job losses in some areas, Whitbread's diversification, especially into retailing, was creating new employment in the company at an even faster rate.

The group was also in the forefront of the movement to help small businesses get off the ground. And the new chairman was pleased to refer to Whitbread's sports sponsorship, which his uncle Bill had begun 30 years before with the Whitbread Gold Cup at Sandown. Other notable Whitbread-sponsored events included Badminton, the Stella Artois Tennis Tournament, the Heineken Ice Hockey Championships and the Whitbread Round-the-World Yacht Race. Nor had the arts been forgotten, with the Whitbread Book of the Year literary award, a rival to the Booker Prize, in its fifteenth year.

Under Simonds-Gooding, Whitbread's organization was formalized into six divisions – Breweries, Trading, Inns, Retail, Wines and Spirits, and North America. Breweries, following the closure of Luton, comprised eight

breweries and two packaging-plants and employed 2,000 people. Trading, responsible for Whitbread's 4,500 tenanted public houses, its free trade, marketing and distribution, had 3,820 employees. Whitbread Inns ran the group's 1,600 managed pubs and employed 20,000. Whitbread Retail had 13,600 employees and included Beefeater, Pizza Hut, Whitbread Coaching Inns, Henekey's Steak Bars, the group's off-licences and Aureon Entertainments, a chain of 33 discothèques. Wines and Spirits incorporated Long John International, the French wine company Calvet, Antinori of Florence, Langenbach and Stowells of Chelsea. And Whitbread North America had grown into a substantial organization embracing the newly-acquired Buckingham Corporation which was being merged with Julius Wile and Fleischmann.

Whitbread International had disappeared from the pantheon, subsumed into North America and Wines and Spirits. So, too, had Soft Drinks, hived off into a company jointly owned by Whitbread and Bass. It was beginning to look as though the group was jelling into its new mould.

But not quite yet. In the middle of 1985, Simonds-Gooding took the board by surprise by leaving to join the advertising group Saatchi & Saatchi. In his place Whitbread appointed Charles Tidbury's protégé Peter Jarvis, previously managing director of Whitbread Trading and a main board member since 1979.

Only 44, Jarvis was a natural choice for the job of managing director. Educated at Bolton School and Cambridge, he had worked for 12 years at Unilever, mostly in Birdseye, in the US and Europe. When Whitbread bought Long John International in 1975, it had hired Jarvis to organize the spirits company's sales and marketing. He had taken over from Simonds-Gooding as group marketing director and since 1980 his main task had been the expansion of Whitbread's European and North American businesses, followed by responsibility for beer sales and tenanted public houses. A private man outside Whitbread, Jarvis had demonstrated a talent for making things run smoothly, an enthusiasm for promoting youth and a dedication to putting the customer first which he said he had learned in North America. 'Shirts coming back from the laundry on hangers, having your shopping carried to your car from the supermarket, high chairs for babies in restaurants, iced water, I remember thinking "if only we could give service like this in the UK, the world would be our oyster."'

The Stella Artois tennis tournament, involving many top players, runs for a week in June.

Peter Jarvis joined Whitbread in 1975 and became group managing director ten years later. He was appointed chief executive in 1990.

133

*The Turf Tavern in Oxford is leased from
Merton College by Whitbread. In the centre
of the city, it can be approached only
through small alleyways.*

CHAPTER ELEVEN

UNIVERSALLY APPROVED

1985–1992

Bringing the history of any organization to a close while it is still in existence is difficult. When, like Whitbread, it is thriving as never before it is all but impossible.

In the seven years since Peter Jarvis became managing director, the group has changed with particular speed. To give just one example, 1987 saw Whitbread's Wines and Spirits division double in size due to the largest takeover in its history, the acquisition of distillers James Burrough, manufacturers of Beefeater Gin, for £174 million. Sam Whitbread reported to shareholders that the deal was extremely exciting as it gave Whitbread a strong foothold in the huge US market for white spirits. James Burrough and Long John International were merged the following March and the two could claim to be fully integrated by 1989 – just in time to be sold to Allied-Lyons, along with Buckingham Wile in the US, for a total of £542 million – a capital profit of something like £300 million on the whole deal.

'As we examined our options,' explained Peter Jarvis, 'it became clear that it would be increasingly difficult for us to become a leading company in wines and spirits internationally. Over the past few years the largest companies in this field have become very much bigger and stronger and it would have required enormous investment on our part to join them.'

The same process had already led to the merger of Langenbach, Calvet and Stowells of Chelsea with Allied-Lyons's wine subsidiary Grants of St James's in a joint venture called European Cellars, as well as a collaborative deal to distribute spirits in the UK.

Jarvis, it was obvious, was not afraid to cut away parts of the group that his predecessors, and he himself, had laboured long and hard to multiply. But what was he going to raise up in their place?

One answer, which his enthusiasm for American standards might have indicated, was restaurants. Pizza Hut had already proved a great success,

TGI (Thank God It's) Friday, an import from the US, has proved to be a popular extension to Whitbread's restaurant group.

with more than 200 branches in the UK and its first branches in Paris doing extraordinarily well. Beefeater restaurants had also topped the 200 mark. Another US import, TGI Friday (TGI stands for Thank God It's, in case you are curious) was also extremely promising. And overseas Whitbread had acquired a Canadian chain of 100 steak and seafood restaurants, which was already expanding into Australia, and a flourishing steak restaurant chain in West Germany. Jarvis was also putting his weight behind Whitbread's hotels and off-licences. And Whitbread's first chief executive, as he had now become, was reaffirming the group's commitments to none other than the manufacture and sale of beer, both through its own pubs and to the free trade.

There had been moments in the last few years when it had seemed conceivable that Whitbread might stop making beer, especially in the light of the Monopolies and Mergers Commission's conclusions at the end of another lengthy investigation of the industry.

The MMC began its most recent investigation of the supply of beer in the UK in 1986, at the prompting of the Office of Fair Trading. Its report was published in March 1989 and concluded that a 'complex monopoly' detrimental to consumer interests did exist in the brewing industry. The MMC said it believed the combination of a few large brewers producing and distributing beer and the tied-house system led to inefficiencies in manufacturing, wholesaling and retailing being passed on to the consumer. The monopoly also prevented real price competition, blocked new companies entering the market and limited consumer choice to the range offered by a single supplier.

This advertisement exemplifies Whitbread's diversification in recent years.

The brewing lobby swung into action. Industry experts pointed out that the six big British brewers only controlled 70 per cent of the UK market, compared with France and Australia, where two brewers accounted for 73 per cent and 90 per cent respectively, and that there were at least another 60 local and regional brewers to provide real competition. Compared to other countries, Britain's pubs offered a greater choice of products, better amenities and some of the lowest retail prices going. What's more, the tied-house system fostered the survival of local and regional brewers and enabled pubs in rural communities to stay open.

It was, of course, special pleading, but it was based on more than two centuries of experience and evolution. Indignantly, the brewers complained that the MMC had not allowed them to challenge its evidence or reply to its charges. The cries were only partially heard and in November 1989 most of the MMC's conclusions became law in the form of the Supply of Beer (Tied Estate) Orders.

These orders required two major changes. From the first of May 1990, the tenants of all tied houses belonging to the major brewers could buy one 'guest' cask ale, and all wines, spirits, ciders, low-alcohol beers and soft drinks, from anyone they liked. And by November 1992, all brewers owning more than 2,000 tied pubs must sell or lease free of the tie half of their pubs above this limit. In the case of Whitbread it meant selling or 'freeing' almost 2,500 pubs.

'These changes are enormously far-reaching,' Jarvis reported to shareholders in June 1990. Angrily, he quoted a pamphlet written by a group of Oxford economists: 'The MMC exhibited an inability to come to terms with the reality of the market-place and produced an economically flawed report. Without pausing to reflect, the Secretary of State committed the Government to implement proposals for a system of permanent regulation of the industry, the likely effects of which the Commission had not even analysed and which, in any case, ran counter to EC Policy.'

Jarvis explained that Whitbread was being forced to rethink its whole relationship with its tenants, as well as cope with the 'gross inefficiencies' the new regulations had imposed on distribution and administration, and the 'considerable turmoil' they had created in the market-place. He put the

Boddington's Bitter and Murphy's Stout 'draughtflow' cans are among the latest developments at Whitbread. Whitbread's White Label is a new low-alcohol bitter.

The Spice Island pub in Portsmouth.

cost to the company at £45 million. 'What a high price to pay for misguided interference.'

He added that while the MMC investigation was under way, Whitbread had determined to continue as a major UK brewer and a significant owner and manager of public houses. The decision to buy Boddington's brewery in Manchester was evidence of this commitment. But the MMC findings hastened the closure of Faversham brewery and Higson's brewery in Liverpool.

A year later Whitbread's reaction to the changes the MMC was imposing on brewers and public houses was more positive. On 1 March 1990 all its beer production, sales and distribution was integrated into a single business called the Whitbread Beer Company. Whitbread Pub Partnerships had already been formed the previous autumn to run the tenanted pubs in compliance with the new Supply of Beer Orders. Whitbread Inns remained responsible for the group's 1,600 managed pubs. Whitbread Restaurants

The Dalmahoy Golf and Country Club close to Edinburgh is one of Whitbread's country club hotels. The house was built by William Adam in 1725 and the two golf courses were designed by James Braid, five times Open champion, in 1920. Two ghosts are said to haunt the old part of the house: a white lady and an old man in a long dark coat.

Wine Rack is one of five distinctive Whitbread brands in high-street drinks retailing.

embraced all the restaurant businesses, which now included 150 Berni Inns bought from Grand Metropolitan. Whitbread Leisure comprised the off-licences, totalling about 1,000 branches mostly trading under the Thresher name, and the hotels, of which there were 74 with another 14 under development.

Peter Jarvis explained that this was the latest refinement in Whitbread's strategy, which was designed to sustain the best of its traditional expertise while positioning the company to compete successfully in the 1990s and beyond.

As a generalization to put to shareholders in an annual report, it was true enough. As an explanation of exactly what Whitbread's position was at the end of 250 years, however, it could perhaps do with a little elaboration.

The truth was that the new legislation arising from the MMC report had weakened the traditional tie between brewers and public houses that had existed throughout the history of Whitbread. Whether that would prove to be a good thing or not for the community at large, only time would tell. But the practical outcome was the forced collapse of the paternal relationship between brewers and the tenants of their pubs.

Although few liked to admit it, the MMC's charges were at least partly justified. The relationship between brewers and the pubs they owned was complicated, to the point where it was almost impossible to pinpoint exactly who benefited most from the links: the brewer, the tenant or the customer. What was also apparent, however, was that the MMC's recommendations were only accelerating what was already happening in the industry.

What Peter Jarvis called Whitbread's strategy was based on its growing appreciation of the changes in its market, not least of all in its pubs, and the company's conviction that the MMC had failed to recognize just how good a deal pubs gave their customers.

Over the last 30 years nearly all the ideals envisaged by Sydney Nevile and other reformers had become at least partial realities in a very large percentage of public houses. Refurbished and welcoming for women as well

Bottoms Up is another off-licence chain. It became part of Whitbread with the acquisition of Peter Dominic in 1991.

Stella Artois is a Belgian lager brewed under licence by Whitbread. A relatively strong lager, it is advertised as being 'reassuringly expensive'.

In the late 1980s Whitbread joined a major new initiative to curb alcohol abuse when it became a founder member of the Portman Group, formed to look into the problem. The company also supported a series of 'drink wisely' posters and other advertisements.

as men, serving food as well as a wide variety of alcoholic and non-alcoholic drinks, many of Whitbread's pubs had been transformed from the stark, male drinking dens they were a generation ago. At long last, too, the restrictions on opening hours imposed in the First World War had given way to all-day opening.

The changes reflected rising public expectations and changing social habits. It was no accident that Whitbread decided its logical line of diversification should be into restaurants and hotels. They weren't just competitors to the public house, they were setting the standards that the pub had to match. People's homes, too, were increasingly comfortable, at least for the majority. To survive, pubs had to be attractive places catering for their local communities, whether they were the Friday evening crowd in the City of London or the Sunday lunch-time gathering in a small village.

The idea of the pub as little more than a tap through which brewers sold their beer had finally had its day. Instead, the pub had to become a profit centre in its own right, a retail outlet with its own margins as distinct from those earned by the manufacturers of the products it stocked as in any shop.

It was a distinction that Whitbread had recognized for more than a hundred years, ever since its bottled beer had first become a national brand. The growth of sales of branded beers and lagers, and of Whitbread's Take-Home Division, in the last 20 years had merely reinforced this knowledge.

But that did not alter the fact that divorcing itself from many of its tied houses at such short notice was a painful business. It was worse for many of its tenants, admittedly. Hard choices had to be made and the terms Whitbread offered were not always acceptable. The bitterness with which Jarvis had greeted the MMC findings was more than echoed in the curses flung at Whitbread's head by some of its tenants when they discovered that the breaking of the 'tie' meant higher rents or the loss of their business – and home – altogether.

Their personal tragedies apart, the outcome of the MMC report was the closure of many local pubs. By the end of the enforced exercise, the total number of on-licences left in the country would be perhaps 60,000, 40 per cent less than a century earlier. Even more dramatic was the decline in the ratio of public houses to population, from 1:300 in 1890 to 1:1000.

This did not reflect a fall in the consumption of beer, or at least not until recently. By 1980 beer consumption in the UK had climbed to more than 40 million barrels, paralleling the growth in population and the rise in disposable incomes. Admittedly, there has been a fall in the last decade to more like 35 million barrels. That in itself, however, has come about partly because pubs have become only one of the places catering to public needs; its competitors including wine bars, fast-food restaurants, steak houses, brasseries, cafés, clubs and hotels of all sorts, shapes and sizes. Not to mention the easy availability of alcoholic drink from off-licences and supermarkets. The latter, in a development which would have astonished earlier generations of Whitbreads, have become the biggest individual retailers of wine, spirits and beer; Whitbread itself owns 1,600 drinks shops.

The availability of alcohol in supermarkets, cheek by jowl with every other domestic consumer product and for sale in an environment open to all, men, women and children, underlines another change in social attitudes which is reflected in Whitbread's business in the 1990s.

If the present Sam Whitbread were to have written a letter to his son about the family brewing business on the 250th anniversary of its founding in 1742, he might well have forecast that the next ten years would see even faster change than had taken place over the last two decades. But he might have been reluctant to say more. The future holds us all hostage. Who, for example, could have forecast the dramatic effect of the recession which in 1991 led to the first fall in Whitbread's profits for 14 years? However, he would still have been justified in observing, in all but the same words as the first Samuel Whitbread two centuries before, that: 'your family has raised it from a very small beginning and by great assiduity in a very long course of years and with the highest credit in every view by honest and fair dealings. And the beer universally approved and the quantity brewed annually great indeed.'

There never was the like before, nor probably ever will be in the Brewing Trade.

The 250th Beefeater restaurant, at Tattenham Corner, opened in February 1992.

The Garrett Street stables finally closed in 1991 and the horses are now kept at Whitbread's hop farm in Kent. A team is brought up to London every year to draw the Lord Mayor's coach for the Show in November.

BIBLIOGRAPHY

The Death of the English Pub – Christopher Hutt (Arrow Books).
Seventy Rolling Years – Sir Sydney O. Nevile (Faber & Faber).
The Brewing Industry in England 1700–1830 – Peter Mathias (Cambridge University Press).
Samuel Whitbread 1764–1815, A Study in Opposition – Roger Fulford (Macmillan).
British Taverns, Their Histories and Laws – Lord Askwith (Routledge).
Southill, A Regency House – (Faber & Faber).
The Creevey Papers – edited by John Gore (Batsford).
A History of the English Public House – H. A. Monckton (Bodley Head).
The Jews in Business – Stephen Aris (Cape).
A History of the Cost of Living – John Burnett (Pelican).
English Society in the Eighteenth Century – Roy Porter (Penguin).
London Life in the Eighteenth Century – M. Dorothy George (Penguin).
Portrait of an Age (Victorian England) – G. M. Young (Oxford University Press).
British Society 1914–45 – John Stevenson (Pelican).
British Society since 1945 – Arthur Marwick (Penguin).
British Social Trends since 1900 – A. H. Halsey (Macmillan).

Two of the Royal Academicians' paintings commissioned by the company in 1937 and 1938. On the left is Oast Houses, Whitbread Hop Farm *by Algernon Talmage; to the right is* The Woolpack Inn *by Stanhope A. Forbes.*

INDEX

(Figures in italics refer to illustrations)

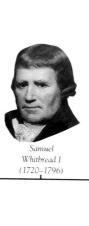

Samuel
Whitbread I
(1720–1796)

Harriot Whitbread
(1785–1832)

Samuel Whitbread II
(1764–1815)

William Henry Whitbread
(1795–1867)

Samuel Charles Whitbread
(1796–1879)

William Whitbread III
(1834–1879)

Samuel Whitbread III
(1830–1895)

Samuel Howard Whitbread
(1858–1944)

Henry William Whitbread
(1861–1947)

Francis Pelham Whitbread
(1867–1941)

Simon Whitbread
(1904–1985)

Col. William Henry Whitbread
(1900–   )

Samuel Charles Whitbread
(1937–   )

*Members of the Whitbread
family who have played a
significant part in the story of
the company.*

Charles [illegible].

F. P. [illegible].

Sydney [illegible]

Robert Sangster

Samuel Whitbread.

[illegible] Browne

Peter Davis.